# Alexander Kennedy

Amazon.com/author/alexanderkennedy

*Copyright © 2017 Fritzen Publishing LLC.
All Rights Reserved.*

*Alexander Kennedy is an imprint owned by Fritzen Publishing LLC.*

*No part of this book may be reproduced or transmitted in any form or by any means, electronic or mechanical, including photocopying, recording or by any information storage and retrieval system, without written permission from the publisher.*

*The information provided within this book is for general informational purposes only. While we try to keep the information up-to-date and correct, there are no representations or warranties, express or implied, about the completeness, accuracy, reliability, suitability or availability with respect to the information, products, services, or related graphics contained in this book for any purpose.*

***Have a question or concern? Let us know.***
FritzenPublishing.com |
support@fritzenpublishing.com

# Contents

Prologue ................................................... 5

Chapter 1: Young Patriot ................................. 13

Chapter 2: Jefferson in the Confederation 49

Chapter 3: The Long Road to the Presidency ................................................................. 87

Chapter 4: The Glorious First Term .......... 127

Chapter 5: Burr, Embargo, and Disaster . 163

Chapter 6: Retirement and Legacy ............ 191

Sources ................................................. 203

# Prologue

In December 1807, Thomas Jefferson announced that he would not seek a third term as president. This seems ordinary to us; we're used to the two-term precedent set by George Washington and followed by every successor save Franklin D. Roosevelt, and finally codified into the Constitution in 1951. But in 1807, only George Washington had renounced a possible third term. Jefferson's immediate predecessor, his irascible rival and former friend John Adams, had been voted out after only one term as president. Had Jefferson desired a third term, the field was clear.

By voluntarily leaving the office after two terms, Washington had famously sought to emulate the Roman general Cincinnatus (namesake of modern Cincinnati, Ohio), who gave up absolute power as dictator of Rome to become a private citizen. In so doing,

Washington set a vital precedent that the American presidency would almost always change hands by election, rather than by the death of the incumbent.

Jefferson's motives were different. He simply didn't think he could win.

His first four years in office had been one of the greatest presidential terms in US history. He made war on and defeated the Barbary pirates who had long preyed on American shipping, a threat even the powerful navy of Great Britain hesitated to engage. He arranged the Louisiana Purchase, buying 828,000 square miles of territory from Napoleon Bonaparte and doubling the size of the United States at a stroke of the pen. He hired Meriwether Lewis and William Clark to lead their famous Corps of Discovery into the West, mapping a huge swath of terrain from

St. Louis to the Pacific Ocean. And despite all these expenses, he cut the national debt by one-third. Unsurprisingly, Jefferson demolished his 1804 challenger Charles Pinckney—a name deservedly forgotten today except by specialist historians—by an electoral vote of 162 to 14.

Yet by the end of his second term, this beloved icon of the American Revolution was receiving death threats by mail and secession threats from Northern politicians. What went so wrong in between?

One problem was Jefferson's scheming former vice president, Aaron Burr. After killing fellow Founding Father Alexander Hamilton in a duel, Burr nonetheless found a way to become even more notorious, trying to pry away a chunk of the Western United States in a military coup. But Jefferson's pursuit of his former running mate for treason was equally unwise, and left his own reputation damaged.

The much bigger problem came down to one word: embargo. After a series of clashes between US and British warships, Jefferson sought to find a way to punish Great Britain and the other European countries embroiled in the Napoleonic Wars.

His "solution" was a disaster. Cutting off his nose to spite his face, Jefferson abandoned his vision of a limited federal government and pressed Congress to declare a virtual stop to American overseas trade. Within a year, the economy was in tatters, smuggling was epidemic, his own party was in revolt against his leadership, and Northern states had begun dangerous whispers about secession. The cause of states' rights had been eviscerated, and its one-time champion had wielded the knife. And by 1812, an unprepared United States would find itself at war with Great Britain anyway—the very outcome Jefferson's policies had been designed to prevent. It was a foreign policy catastrophe no other president has yet matched; even disasters like the Vietnam or Iraq Wars never posed an existential threat to the nation.

Appropriately, historians have always had trouble assessing the elusive Jefferson, and few presidents have seen so many ups and downs in their historical reputations. The "big three" of Abraham Lincoln, George Washington, and Franklin Roosevelt have almost always been lionized, save for a few conservative dissenters in the latter case. Jefferson's popular image more complicated—sometimes placed in their illustrious company, and sometimes not.

Jefferson's reputation rose throughout his life—not steadily, but in fits and starts, like any public figure. By his death in 1826, he was remembered as one of the great figures of the revolutionary generation. But during and after the Civil War, his creation of the doctrine of states' rights seemed pernicious to many, and his stock plummeted. Turn-of-the-century historians like Henry Adams disparaged him, and progressive Democratic president Woodrow Wilson called him "not a great American."

It was FDR and the New Deal Democrats that salvaged his reputation, making him a symbol of their "common man" populism. Jefferson became one of America's favorite presidents once more, only to see another reverse in the 1960s when his hypocrisy over slavery, particularly his sexual involvement with one of his slaves, became a major issue. In late

2015, students at University of Missouri at Columbia and the College of William & Mary even attempted to have statues of Jefferson removed from their campuses.

This book seeks neither to bury Jefferson nor to praise him, but rather to take a middle road between these extremes. It will explore how a leader of such evident talents—even greatness—could lead his country almost to the point of its own destruction. Much of the problem lay in Jefferson's philosophy and even personality, and to see the origins of both, we must first turn to his early life.

# Chapter 1: Young Patriot

# The Shadwell Fire

On February 1, 1770, Thomas Jefferson's birthplace in Shadwell, Virginia burned to the ground. Jefferson was twenty-seven at the time, and saw the fire as a calamity. Besides losing most of his books—£200 worth, a fabulous sum in those days—he also lost every letter and record in his possession.

Biographers have had similar reasons to rue this fire, which destroyed so much evidence about Jefferson's early life. An obsessive writer, Jefferson documented the rest of his life with torrents of letters, detailed farm books, and other records. He was not above altering these records for posterity from time to time; historians have found multiple instances where he modified or excised opinions that seemed to him foolish in hindsight. Nor was he above omitting crucial matters entirely, such as the six children he probably had with his slave Sally Hemings (a controversy this book will discuss in more detail in Chapter Two).

Still, the documentary record Jefferson left is extraordinary, one that few historical figures can match—but only for the years after the Shadwell Fire. Before 1770, in contrast, biographers can only sketch his life in broad strokes, and much of the young Jefferson is lost to us.

## Origins

Jefferson was born into a wealthy family—or at least, a family in the debt-ridden but outwardly luxurious class that passed for "wealthy" in colonial Virginia. His father, Peter Jefferson, was the archetype of the colonial self-made man, a hard-working planter, surveyor, and autodidact who steadily expanded his holdings in both property and enslaved human beings. In his lifetime, Peter was best known for having teamed with a professor named Joshua Fry to draw the first accurate map of Virginia; he also served in the Virginia House of Burgesses. Thomas spoke proudly of his father in later life, though little documentary evidence exists about him beyond Thomas's recollections (the Shadwell fire problem again). Peter died in 1757, when Thomas was fourteen.

In 1739, Peter had married Jane Randolph, a woman from one of Virginia's leading families. The pair had nine children, the third of which was Thomas, born 1743. Thomas's relationship with his mother has long puzzled historians. He rarely spoke of her, and there is some evidence he kept his distance from her in the years before her 1776 death. Biographer

Merrill Peterson even wrote that she had "zero" role in Jefferson's emotional life, though this extreme statement hardly seems likely. Given the near-total lack of documentary evidence, historians seem unlikely to ever resolve if Jefferson was estranged from his mother somehow, or merely had the lack of interest in his mother so common in men of the revolutionary generation. At most, we can say that the two do not appear to have been close.

## Childhood

Jefferson's own earliest memory, to the amusement or chagrin of generations of scholars, was of being carried on a pillow by a slave as the family moved from his Shadwell birthplace to Tuckahoe in 1745. His eight siblings appear to have been unexceptional. One of them died in infancy; one of them was a mentally disabled girl who would later wander from the house and die in a thunderstorm as a young woman; none of them left a significant record behind.

But Thomas was different. He learned the violin at a young age, studied Latin and Greek at home with tutors, and at age nine was enrolled by his father in a private school. Jefferson was miserable away from home and cared little for his teacher, a Goochland County pastor. His father's death was a great trauma to the fourteen-year-old boy; Thomas was the eldest son, and felt abandoned and suddenly thrust into maturity. He switched schools, enrolling in an Albemarle County private school twelve miles from Shadwell, where his family again lived. He deepened his understanding of Greek and Latin there, but more importantly, could visit his family on the weekends. Jefferson claimed later in life that he fell in with "bad company" for a while after his father's death, but this appears to have been an old man's embellishments. The truth was that Jefferson was well provided for, inheriting 5,000 acres and a multitude of slaves, and despite his remarkable gifts, could never rightly be called a "self-made man."

Even as Jefferson learned the violin and classical languages, he also learned his way around the Virginia wilderness. This odd blend of pioneer and aristocrat, which would later so delight Parisian society, was instilled in his character early. His father taught him to ride, to track, and to hunt. Well into his old age, long after his family had tried to insist he should stop, Jefferson went for a long daily ride around his property.

# Williamsburg

In 1760, at the age of seventeen, Jefferson went to Williamsburg to attend the College of William & Mary. Williamsburg had 1,500 residents at the time, which seemed to the rural Jefferson to be a large city. Always a bookish boy, Jefferson now had the chance to throw himself into intellectual life as never before. Here he also fell in love for the first time (with Rebecca Burwell, the sister of a friend, who did not return his feelings), and he implied in correspondence that he lost his virginity as well (though certainly not with Rebecca Burwell; biographer Jon Meacham speculates that he most likely had an involvement with a slave or a servant girl). When Burwell married another man, Jefferson retreated to his bed with one of the headaches that would plague him at moments of crisis throughout his life. He called them migraines, though they do not appear to have been migraines in the modern medical sense, but rather the intense psychosomatic manifestations of a sensitive man's stress.

Most importantly for Jefferson's future, though, he met George Wythe.

# George Wythe

George Wythe was a lawyer and prominent Virginia gentleman who introduced the precocious young man to a more rarified society, often bringing Jefferson along to dine with the colonial governor. Jefferson's personal ambitions began to grow accordingly. After his graduation in 1762, Wythe employed him as a clerk while he studied the law. Jefferson being Jefferson, he not only read the law, but everything else he could get his hands on, familiarizing himself with Enlightenment figures like Immanuel Kant, John Locke, Isaac Newton, and Francis Bacon. He also read deeply into British history. It was probably during these years that his idiosyncratic belief was born that all world history could be summarized as a repeated struggle between tyrannical Tory elites and Whig popular movements.

Wythe's life would later come to a sad end in 1806, during Jefferson's presidency. He had adopted a free-born mixed-race boy named Michael Brown, widely rumored to be his own illegitimate son, and had fixed most of his property on the young man in his will. One day, a visiting grandson of his sister's apparently poisoned and killed both Wythe and Brown with their morning coffee, hoping to inherit Wythe's property for himself. He was acquitted of Wythe's murder, and the charges for Brown's murder were dismissed by judges because of the victim's mixed race. As we will later see again with Jefferson's father-in-law, Jefferson was surrounded by male role models who made little secret of their apparent slave concubines.

# T. Jefferson, Attorney-at-Law

But for now, the Wythe tragedy and scandal lay far in the future. Jefferson became a member of the Virginia Bar in 1767 and had his first client in February of that year. Jefferson was never much of an orator, either as a lawyer or a politician, but he won a reputation for his conscientious preparation and deep knowledge of the law. He soon was handling as many as five hundred cases a year, and would continue to do so throughout the early 1770s. With a growing reputation among the Virginia elite—and his family connection to Speaker of the House Peyton Randolph on his mother's side—Jefferson was easily elected to the Virginia House of Burgesses in 1769, where he would serve until his election to the Second Continental Congress.

During this period, he also began construction of Monticello, his famous hilltop residence. (The name is Italian for "little mountain.") Jefferson was a student of architecture, as he was in so many subjects. He was deeply influenced by the Palladian style then popular in Europe, which in turn drew heavily on Greek and Roman models. "Roman" civic virtues were an important influence on many Founding Fathers—many openly longed to be the Cicero of their generation—and the architectural reflection of these virtues can be seen from Monticello to the US Capitol to Jefferson's later work at the University of Virginia.

Unlike the others, Monticello would never be more than half-finished. His later travels in Europe as Ambassador to France gave Jefferson a new appreciation of Palladian architecture, and when he returned, he tore down almost everything to begin anew. Every time he completed one section, he ripped down another in an endless cycle. Visitors would often find piles of bricks of lumber strewn about or even missing walls or roofs. Biographer Joseph J. Ellis recounts stories that at times Jefferson had more than a hundred people working on the house—some of them hired hands, some of them his own slaves.

## Martha

In 1770, Jefferson's heart had sufficiently recovered from the Rebecca Burwell disaster to begin courting a pretty young widow, Martha Wayles Skelton, who had a three-year-old son. He was in a position to court far more confidently than he had with Burwell: a lawyer of growing reputation and wealth, a seasoned man of twenty-six who had traveled outside of his own colony (somewhat rare in those days of bad roads), and a delegate to the House of Burgesses.

No portrait of Martha survives, nor any of her letters—a heartbroken Jefferson burned these after her death, his own personal Shadwell fire. But we know that Jefferson was deeply in love and eager to marry. Only the destruction of Shadwell and the slow construction of Monticello prevented him from proposing; though he had a woman he wanted for a bride, and who apparently wanted him back, he had nowhere yet to put her or a family. The two courted for fifteen months, finally marrying on New Year's Day, 1772. Their first child, a girl also named Martha who went by "Patsy," was born nine months later. Jefferson would later look back on his tragically short time with Martha as the happiest years of his life.

Martha's apparently wealthy father, John Wayles, died only a year after the marriage. Through Martha, Jefferson was his inheritor—married women were not allowed to own or inherit property in their own name under Virginia law—and the young man handled the situation disastrously. Though Wayles owned wide swaths of property and more than a hundred slaves, he also had a good deal of red in his ledger; his lands had been used as collateral on several outstanding loans. Rather than simply settling the debts by selling off most of the land, Jefferson opted instead to inherit both land and debt together, in the hope that he could make sufficient profit from the lands to settle the debt later. He never would, and from 1773 until his death, Jefferson would be increasingly, sometimes desperately, in debt.

But for the nonce, Jefferson became one of the largest slaveholders in Virginia. Among the slaves that Jefferson inherited were six of his wife's half-brothers and half-sisters, the mixed-race children of John Wayles. These half-siblings were given privileged positions around Monticello, trained in trades and housework, and spared the worst of the heavy labor of the fields. The youngest of them, only an infant at the time of Wayles' death, was a girl named Sally Hemings.

## Rumors of War

Though he would have done well to focus his attention on sorting out his financial affairs at this time, Jefferson's attention was increasingly drawn to the international stage.

In the more than one hundred and fifty years since their founding, the American colonies had had a cordial relationship with their "mother country" of Great Britain. No significant rebellion had been seen since Leisler's Rebellion took over New York in 1689, and even that had been the result of a brief civil war (the "Glorious Revolution") on the British mainland, rather than an indigenous American movement.

But by the 1760s and '70s, that cordiality was rapidly fraying. The global conflict known as the Seven Years' War—called the "French and Indian War" in the colonies—had left Great Britain the undisputed master of the world stage, but also heavily in debt. In the first sign of trouble, large numbers of British troops, popularly known as "redcoats" for their distinctive uniforms, had been left behind in the colonies after the fight with the French was over. With these troops, King George III saw an opportunity to assert more control over his wayward possessions.

One immediately unpopular measure banned colonial settlers from crossing the Appalachians into territory newly won in the Seven Years' War. Though owned by France and then by Britain on European maps, the area was in fact populated by many Native American tribes, with whom the British wanted no further trouble for now. (A sad pattern of early US–Native American relations is that many Native American tribes, who had no illusions about the expansionist intentions of their new white neighbors, readily allied with anyone who would make war on them; once victorious, the white settlers of the Americas saw these alliances as justification for further seizure of Native American-held lands.) Britain had no particular humanitarian motives here, only a desire to avoid paying for further wars, but by blocking the American expansionist impulse, it created a broad demographic eager for an end to imperial rule.

## Taxes

But the greatest issue was taxes. The tax burden of the average colonist had historically been far lower than that of the average Englishman. This stemmed both from the difficulties of collecting taxes across an ocean and from a willingness to allow the colonies some measure of self-government.

The Seven Years' War changed the mood in Britain dramatically, however. The country had spent massively to defend its American colonies against France; why should this burden be borne by those living in England, rather than in the disputed area? After the colonies declined the opportunity to raise the demanded money through their own means, the British Parliament passed the 1765 Stamp Act, the first direct tax on the colonies.

Popular opinion polls of course did not exist at the time, nor would they have been heeded if they had. But at least a vocal minority of colonists was outraged. Massachusetts lawyer James Otis, a hero of future US President John Adams, coined the famous phrase "no taxation without representation," referring to the lack of colonial representation in the parliament passing these taxes. (The British responded imaginatively that the colonies had "virtual representation" from conscientious MPs, and needed no actual representatives.) Groups like the Sons of Liberty were formed to protest and riot, even destroying the house of the Royal Governor of Massachusetts, James

Hutchinson. The government of British Prime Minister George Grenville fell, and led by his successor, the Marquess of Rockingham, the new Parliament repealed the Stamp Act.

But the debt problem was not going anywhere. In 1767, Parliament tried again with the Townshend Acts, taxing paper, tea, and other goods. More riots resulted, one of which culminated in a group of British soldiers firing into a crowd that was stoning them, the so-called "Boston Massacre." In Virginia, the House of Burgesses passed a resolution joining an embargo against "Townshend goods," and called on Jefferson to draft it. These Acts were likewise repealed, except for the tax on tea. In 1773, this led to more trouble when John Adams' cousin Samuel led a group of patriots to dump a massive cargo of tea into Boston Harbor, more than a million dollars of damage in today's currency. Parliament responded with the Coercive Acts, a series of heavily punitive measures on Massachusetts alone.

Meanwhile, in Virginia, the movement for independence was being led not by Jefferson, but by perhaps the greatest orator of his generation, Patrick Henry, famous for his later demand of "Give me liberty or give me death." Influenced by Henry, Wythe, and others, Jefferson was increasingly coming to see greater colonial autonomy, if not outright independence, as not just a necessary step but the inevitable forward march of history.

## Colonial Congress

Jefferson missed his shot at the First Colonial Congress for the usual reason. He had prepared assiduously to be a member of Virginia's delegation, drafting a long criticism of the British Parliament that he wished to present. But on the way to the House of Burgesses session that would select the delegates, he was felled by another of his stress headaches. He missed both the session and his chance to go to Philadelphia.

Still, his effort was not entirely wasted. His allies in the Virginia Assembly published his writings without his knowledge as A Summary View of the Rights of British America. It appeared in early 1775, after the first shots had been fired at Lexington, Concord, and Bunker Hill, and was an immediate hit both for its timing and his skillful prose. His eloquent defense of the colonies' right to self-government was the start of his national reputation.

In 1775, the Virginia Assembly was again selecting delegates to the Constitutional Convention, and this time Jefferson managed to stay on his feet. He was not chosen in the first round, but named an alternate. When his relative, Speaker of the House Peyton Randolph, was recalled to Virginia by the royal governor, Jefferson took Randolph's place in Philadelphia.

# First Declaration

Never much of a speaker, Jefferson said almost nothing during his year as a delegate, but the Congress recognized his talent as a writer and put him to work accordingly. He had barely arrived when he was asked to draft a "Declaration on the Causes and Necessity of Taking Up Arms." He did as asked, but his version was heavily watered down by the then-dominant peace party led by Pennsylvania delegate John Dickinson.

Despite befriending Benjamin Franklin and John Adams, after some months in Philadelphia, Jefferson began to long to return home. In those days before "the United States" existed, most Americans considered their state their "native country" rather than their nation; not until after the Civil War would people begin to refer to "the United States" as a singular entity rather than a plural one. Jefferson longed to be in his own country, Virginia, in this crucial hour, and he was also concerned about his wife's poor health. But before he left, the Congress had one more writing task for him. Ironically, in the light of later history, it was a job that no one else seemed to want.

## Second Declaration

By mid-1776, the independence movement was a juggernaut, and Dickinson's coalition was in retreat. (Even Dickinson himself would later serve as an officer in the revolutionary army.) With some instigation by Adams and Franklin, Richard Henry Lee of Virginia made a motion on June 7, 1776 for the colonies to declare independence. While Congress debated the measure, a drafting committee was formed to write the declaration itself, consisting of Adams, Franklin, Roger Sherman of Connecticut, Robert Livingston of New York, and Jefferson, who was appointed both as an available Virginian—Lee was returning to Williamsburg—and as an able writer.

The committee then debated who would draw up the first draft, which was seen as a thankless labor as opposed to the more urgent task of marshalling the actual votes for independence. Adams correctly insisted that he was too "obnoxious, suspected, and unpopular" to wield the pen himself, and that in any case the

Declaration would win more support from the Southern delegations if a Virginian was its author. Jefferson retired to his boarding house and began work. Over the next seventeen days, he would produce one of the seminal documents of American history.

When the Continental Congress took up debate of the document some weeks later, they characteristically missed the point, spending most of their time debating Jefferson's list of complaints against George III. Listening to this debate of his words was a misery for the sensitive author, and Franklin reports Jefferson writhing as the debate unfolded. For the rest of his life, he would circulate his original draft as the "real" Declaration.

But what made the Declaration so important, and Jefferson deservedly one of the great human rights heroes of the modern age, was not the list of grievances against the king, though he wrote this section with his usual felicity. What launched Jefferson into history was the astonishing preface: "We hold these truths to be self-evident, that all men are created equal, that they are endowed by their Creator with certain unalienable Rights, that among these are Life, Liberty and the pursuit of Happiness." With these words, Jefferson transformed a general statement of grievances into a philosophical tract on the rights of human beings. With these words, he stamped the American Revolution not as a mere change of dynasties, like England's Glorious Revolution of a century before, but as a fundamental turning point in world history, after which government would increasingly come only with the consent of the governed.

These ideas had been expressed before, particularly in the works of Enlightenment philosophers and George Mason's recent Virginia Declaration of Rights, which declared:

That all men are born equally free and independent, and have certain inherent natural Rights, of which they cannot by any Compact, deprive or divest their Posterity; among which are the Enjoyment of Life and Liberty, with the Means of acquiring and possessing Property, and pursuing and obtaining Happiness and Safety.

But Jefferson brought these ideas to the national stage, and gave them their most eloquent formulation to date.

In the chaos of an unfolding revolution, few had time to stop and fully appreciate Jefferson's achievement, even the man himself. Jefferson's authorship was not even public knowledge until 1784. And had Jefferson died on his way back home to Virginia, history might have only the same one-note memory of him that it does of Richard Henry Lee, who made the successful motion for independence, or Paul Revere, who rode through the night to warn the militias of Lexington and Concord. Yet as Jefferson's political role and faction grew in later years, allowing his ideas to take greater hold, the Declaration was increasingly viewed as a key moment in the American Revolution, perhaps even the key moment. It was the first of the three achievements Jefferson would later request to have engraved on his tombstone.

## Slavery and the Declaration

Many commentators from Jefferson's day to this have seen some irony in one of America's leading owners of enslaved people writing that "all men are created equal." (An equal number of commentators, starting with John Adams's wife Abigail, have also noted that Jefferson's conception excluded women from these rights.)

Jefferson had abundant rationalizations for his slaveholding at every stage of his career, which evolved as he grew older. In fairness to Jefferson and other slave-owning founding fathers, they found themselves in a difficult position; though they recognized the system in which they lived to be evil, it was difficult to extricate themselves from it. Slaves accounted for much of their personal wealth and formed the basis of their local economy. To free their slaves meant inventing a whole new way of life for themselves at a time when social mobility was much less than today.

A close analogy can be made with today's climate change debate. A majority of Americans agree with the scientific consensus that anthropogenic climate change is one of the greatest threats facing the world, and these people recognize both the immediate suffering from record hurricanes, droughts, and forest fires and in the long-term effects on future generations. Yet how many Americans with these beliefs have given up the cars around which our economy is organized, or even taken the simpler step of eating less meat? Rather than be individual pioneers in radical sacrifice, most Americans (and most people around the world) prefer to wait for society-wide solutions such as new mass transportation systems, a power grid fueled by renewable energy sources, and electric cars.

This parallels Jefferson's situation almost exactly. He despised slavery and believed an improved future society would abolish it, but he believed, or at least claimed to believe, that individual slave owners personally emancipating their slaves made little difference. It might even do harm to black and white alike, by creating a population of illiterate, second-class citizens with no ready work and a deep resentment against the ruling class. Like every American president up through Abraham Lincoln, Jefferson found it impossible to imagine a biracial, much less multiracial, society living in peace; freedom for blacks could easily mean death for whites. In 1820, Jefferson would write to a correspondent, "As it is, we have the wolf by the ear, and we can neither hold him, nor safely let him go. Justice is in one scale, and self-preservation in the other."

For this, Jefferson blamed George III. It was not a very coherent argument, but the best that he could muster under the circumstances. Jefferson tended to see the world in dichotomies, which meant that any evil had to stem from a corrupt European aristocracy, rather than "innocent" young America; in the words of biographer Joseph J. Ellis, "slavery was the serpent in the garden sent there by a satanic king." Jefferson could thus write in the Declaration with a straight face that slavery was "cruel war against nature itself" and a reflection of European corruption, rather than having anything to do with the greed of American planters like himself. He then added, with a hypocrisy noted even in his day, a protest against British officers who called for enslaved blacks to fight against their rebellious white masters in exchange for their freedom.

The Continental Congress had little patience for watching the young Virginian tie himself in rhetorical knots over this issue. The language about slavery was struck from the final draft.

# Chapter 2: Jefferson in the Confederation

# Return to Virginia

In September 1776, having made what seemed like only a modest contribution on the national stage, Jefferson followed his heart and returned to his home "country" of Virginia. He was named a colonel of the militia and re-elected to the Virginia House of Delegates, the successor to the House of Burgesses in the new state government.

Jefferson hadn't made it quite in time to help draft the state constitution, though they did add some of his language from the Declaration of Independence as a preamble. Having missed this moment to make his mark, Jefferson turned to important issues of legal reform one by one.

One lasting mark that he made on Virginia society was to abolish entail, the law that forbade the division of large, aristocratic estates. In England, this law had meant that first-born sons generally inherited all of their father's holdings, while younger siblings had to make their fortunes by marriage or in professions such as the military or the clergy. By striking down this requirement in Virginia, Jefferson inadvertently encouraged the creation of a robust middle class; rather than a small, invariable number of large estates, the estates tended to be divided among children over time, gradually distributing the wealth rather than concentrating it in a small aristocracy.

In all, Jefferson wrote 126 bills in three years, often with the assistance of his old mentor George Wythe, still some years away from being murdered by his coffee. Most of their bills were ignored by the legislature, but one important measure was passed establishing general education, which Jefferson believed necessary for an informed citizenry to participate in the rapidly expanding democratic process.

## Religious Liberty

Jefferson also pushed for a bill guaranteeing religious liberty in the state, which proved to be a harder fight. Many states restricted or banned some religious practices into the early nineteenth century; though the ratification of the First Amendment to the US Constitution guaranteed that the federal government would not interfere with religious freedom, the provisions of the Bill of Rights would not be applied to the states until the twentieth century. In 1776, Virginia's official religion was Anglicanism, though it was renamed the Episcopalian Church that year for obvious reasons. But the Church had weakened its position by siding against the rebellious elements in the colonies, and by the infamous corruption of its ministers.

Jefferson's own religious views were complex and private. Raised Christian, he believed in both God and Christ, though he felt that the Bibles stories of miracles and other divine appearances were simply superstition. Rather, like many Enlightenment figures, Jefferson held to "deism," the belief that God had set the universe and its laws in motion like a master clockmaker, and after that instant had no need to further interfere.

Later in life, he assembled a personal Bible, literally cutting and pasting verses into what seemed to him a more sensible version. In one letter, Jefferson referred to the Four Evangelists as "ignorant, unlettered men," whose writings were full of "superstitions, fanaticisms, and fabrications." In his own Bible, Jefferson eliminated almost all moments of supernatural occurrences, including the resurrection of Christ, but kept the doctrines of Jesus intact. Jefferson rarely spoke or wrote to others of his religious beliefs, however, surely aware of the political danger of putting his unorthodox views into writing. As we shall see, charges of "atheism" later became a major Federalist talking point when he sought national office.

With these idiosyncratic personal beliefs, it's unsurprising that Jefferson became a major advocate for freedom of conscience. In 1802, he famously advocated "a wall of separation between Church & State," a phrase often cited in later decisions of the United States Supreme Court. A true religion, he argued, had no need of a government to defend it: "The legitimate powers of government extend to such acts only as are injurious to others. But it does me no injury for my neighbour to say there are twenty gods, or no god. It neither picks my pocket nor breaks my leg. ... Reason and free enquiry are the only effectual agents against error."

To Jefferson's disappointment, his Virginia Statute for Religious Freedom failed to pass either in 1776 or the following year. But he had begun a decade-long argument in which he and his new ally James Madison would eventually triumph. In 1786, while Jefferson was in France, Madison reintroduced the bill to the Virginia legislature and passed it after a bitter struggle with conservative forces headed by Patrick Henry. The statute was one of the first of its kind, and both the bill and its author were hailed by Enlightenment figures across America and Europe. This was the second accomplishment that Jefferson would one day ask to have engraved on his tombstone.

## Governor

In 1779, Jefferson's allies arranged for him to be elected Virginia's governor. It appeared to be the capstone to his political career; the office of President of the United States did not yet exist, and Jefferson's interests then much more local than global. His two terms as governor would be far from illustrious, however.

Governor Jefferson continued fighting to reform the laws on religious freedom, education, and inheritance. He also moved the state capital from Williamsburg to Richmond, where it remains today. In 1780, he was elected without difficulty to a second one-year term.

But at the very end of that year, the famous American traitor Benedict Arnold invaded Virginia, now at the head of 1,600 redcoats. Jefferson hesitated in the face of conflicting reports and held off for a crucial two days before summoning militia to defend Richmond. Though Jefferson summoned enough men to outnumber Arnold three to one, he had not given them enough time to make the trip over Virginia's frozen roads, and Arnold sacked Richmond unopposed as the government fled. Jefferson's home as governor was among the targets of British looters. General Cornwallis then sent forces after Jefferson at Monticello; Jefferson escaped capture, while some of his enslaved workers used the presence of British soldiers to escape their own captivity.

Even as these events transpired, the Virginia Assembly was selecting Jefferson's successor.

Though Jefferson's flights had been reasonable—his capture would have done the Revolution no good—he made his actions appear much worse by refusing to come to the temporary new capital at Staunton to formally turn power over to his successor, resulting in a brief interregnum in a moment of statewide crisis. Charges of cowardice would dog him for the rest of his political life.

In the following years, the Virginia Assembly convened an inquiry into Jefferson's loss of Richmond and other actions. The inquiry vindicated his actions, concluding that even immediate action could not have stopped Arnold's forces and that Jefferson had been right to flee rather than risk capture and leave the state leaderless. But the inquiry and public criticism that accompanied it left Jefferson badly scarred. Almost no American president has had a temperament less suited to the rough-and-tumble of politics than the sensitive, insecure Jefferson—only Richard Nixon can truly compete with him in this regard.

Jefferson wrote to another new ally, James Monroe, that he was done with politics for good after this experience. The psychic wounds he had suffered, he claimed, would only "be cured by the all-healing grave."

# Notes

Retired back to Monticello, seemingly for good, Jefferson launched into a major scholarly project that he would title Notes on the State of Virginia. The project had its origin in an inquiry from the French diplomat François Barbé-Marbois about the conditions in each of the thirteen American states. Jefferson used Barbé-Marbois's questions as the starting point for his text, which quickly swelled to book-length.

In keeping with the breadth of Jefferson's interests, his treatment is comprehensive. He discusses Virginia's legal system, which he had had a hand in shaping; he discusses farming conditions, which he had experienced firsthand; he catalogues the flora and fauna, drawing on his wanderings in the Virginia wilderness. He also makes an extended argument for the virtue of farmers over manufacturers and other segments of the economy:

Those who labour in the earth are the chosen people of God, if ever he had a chosen people, whose breasts he has made his peculiar deposit for substantial and genuine virtue. It is the focus in which he keeps alive that sacred fire, which otherwise might escape from the face of the earth. Corruption of morals in the mass of cultivators is a phaenomenon of which no age nor nation has furnished an example.

But Notes is most of interest to the modern reader as a detailed examination of both slavery and racial issues. As elsewhere, Jefferson speaks well of American indigenous peoples, calling them the equals of whites. But he believed people of African descent to be intellectually and physically inferior from birth, and in these pages, his racism takes its most explicit form; he even writes of what he considered the unpleasant smell of African Americans.

These virulent views were of course widely held among whites of Jefferson's day, on both sides of the slavery debate. For example, later president and famous anti-slavery leader John Quincy Adams (who as a young man knew

Jefferson well) commented after a performance of Othello that "it served Desdemona right for marrying a nigger." But Jefferson did have contemporaries who suggested that the apparently limited capacities of enslaved Africans and African Americans were only a result of their brutal environment and lack of opportunity—Jefferson's great rival Alexander Hamilton argued exactly this. For a man so dedicated to tearing down conventional wisdom in other arenas, it is disappointing that Jefferson chose to repeat this obvious nonsense.

The discussion of slavery in Notes, on the other hand, is startling for its moral clarity. Jefferson is unambiguous that slavery is a "great political and moral evil" that must be restricted and eventually abolished. "Indeed I tremble for my country when I reflect that God is just." He argues as before, however, that the former slaves must be settled in a far western territory or returned to Africa, because the two races would inevitably fall to bloodshed living side by side: "the real distinctions which nature has made, and many other circumstances, will divide us into parties, and produce convulsions which will probably never end but in the extermination of the one or the other race."

Notes on the State of Virginia was ironically first published in Paris in 1785, during Jefferson's diplomatic service. But copies quickly found their way back to America, and reception was not what Jefferson had hoped for. Reactions to the book generally focused on the passages about slavery, and while John Adams and other Northerners enthused about Jefferson's denunciations, his Virginia neighbors were less pleased. After this publication, Jefferson disappeared from the front lines of the fight against slavery and would never re-appear. Nor would he ever try to publish another book, preferring instead to disseminate his views through endless letter writing, allowing him to carefully tailor each statement of his beliefs to the intended recipient.

# Widower

Like any large family of the day, whether rich or poor, the Jeffersons were familiar with tragedy. Thomas was barely a teenager when he lost his father, and he had lost several of his siblings over the years. In 1771, he and Martha lost a four-year-old son; in 1775, they lost a daughter not yet one year old; in 1781, they lost an infant daughter named Lucy Elizabeth; in 1784, Thomas would lose a three-year-old daughter to whom he had given the same name. But the most devastating tragedy of his life was the death of Martha herself in 1782, only a year after the apparent end of his political career.

Martha's health had never been robust, and several previous childbirths had nearly killed her; her mother had died in childbirth as well. Though Thomas clearly adored his wife, it does not speak well of his foresight that the couple continued to have children after so many brushes with death. After the birth of the second Lucy Elizabeth in August 1782, Martha was ill and bedbound for three weeks before she finally passed.

Oral tradition holds that Martha made Thomas swear a promise to her that if she died, he would never remarry, apparently because she feared that a stepmother might mistreat her children. If true, this was a moment with profound implications for

Martha's unacknowledged half-sister Sally Hemings, now nine years old. Whatever the case, Jefferson did remain legally a bachelor for the remainder of his life.

When Martha finally passed, Thomas was so stricken with grief that he had to be carried from the room by slaves. For months he wandered aimlessly over the grounds of Monticello, sometimes sobbing, always inconsolable.

But even as Jefferson grieved, the new national congress, formed under the Articles of Confederation, continued to ask him for help. With behind the scenes prodding from James Madison, some of his friends hoped (rightly) that new duties and a change of scene could help bring Jefferson back from his despair. But even more, they knew that the young country could not afford to waste a man of Jefferson's talents.

Jefferson was appointed a minister plenipotentiary to help negotiate the peace treaty with Great Britain, which had suffered what would prove its final defeat of the Revolutionary War at Yorktown the year before. But before Jefferson could leave, word returned that Benjamin Franklin, John Adams, and John Jay had already finalized a stellar treaty recognizing American independence. Jefferson would remain in America for another year after all.

# Congress of the Confederation

The Articles of Confederation, first drafted in 1777, had finally been ratified in 1781 after some territorial claims between the states had been settled. A national government finally existed, though events would prove it to be a fatally weak one. Without taxation powers, the Confederation struggled to maintain even a small budget for national defense, and without a strong executive, negotiations with foreign powers were difficult to impossible.

Jefferson was elected to a seat in the Congress of the Confederation in 1783, the second national legislature in which he had served. Though he served in this body for only a year, he made several decisions of lasting importance. First, he helped establish US currency on a decimal basis, sparing centuries of American schoolchildren the trouble of learning to convert pounds to shillings to pence. (Britain, in contrast, would not convert to a decimal system until 1971.)

More importantly, he wrote the basis of what would become the Land Ordinance of 1784, which dictated how America's western territories would be settled and new states admitted to the union. (This act in turn became the famous Northwest Ordinance of 1787.) Jefferson's proposed state names were famously odd, mishmashes of Latin and indigenous languages like Assenisipia, Polypotamia, Pelisipia, and Cherronesus. But his plan was sensible on the whole and provided the means for thirty-seven more states to eventually enter the union, as well as the rectangular grid along which so many state counties would later be formed.

Jefferson also made another attempt to hold the line on slavery, proposing a ban on slaveholding in all future US territories and states. This blanket ban was rejected for the country as a whole, but became law for the

Northwest Territories. The ban was called the "Jefferson Proviso."

# France

In 1784, Jefferson was named the American Minister to France. In this role, he would be succeeding Benjamin Franklin, who had made himself into a beloved popular phenomenon whose likeness was sold on every street corner. Jefferson was aware of the shoes he would have to fill; when the French foreign minister Vergennes said to Jefferson, "You replace Monsieur Franklin, I hear," Jefferson replied, "I succeed him. No man can replace him." Jefferson arrived in Paris in August 1784, and Franklin resigned the post and passed it to Jefferson a few months later.

Jefferson never attained quite the same social success as Franklin. Realistically, no one could have, though Jefferson was further hampered by his lack of proficiency in spoken French. Always more comfortable with writing than face-to-face interaction, Jefferson could read and write passable French but simply could not seem to attain spoken fluency.

During these years, Jefferson became close with his one-time colleague John Adams, who was serving as the American Minister to Great Britain; John's wife Abigail; and their oldest son John Quincy. The diplomatic assignments of the two men prefigured many of the issues that would later split them. Though both disliked the British monarch George III, Adams rediscovered his admiration for many aspects of British administration and government, while Jefferson's exposure to French revolutionary ideals would deepen his faith in the radical aspects of the American experiment.

Jefferson also brought with him Martha's enslaved half-brother, James Hemings, to train as a French chef. On returning to America, Jefferson and Hemings would do much to popularize French cuisine. Jefferson's spendthrift habits took on new impetus during his Paris years as he developed new tastes for expensive French wines and books, both of which he would continue to have shipped to him throughout his life. Aside from the Hemings family, this debt would prove to be of serious consequence for the enslaved people of Monticello.

## Head vs. Heart

Unexpectedly to Jefferson but expectedly to anyone aware of Paris's reputation, Jefferson also fell in love. The subject of his adoration was Maria Cosway, a young and beautiful English artist. Unfortunately, Cosway was also married, to the great Regency Era portrait painter Richard Cosway.

Jefferson and Maria Cosway were introduced by John Trumbull, the artist who painted the image of the Declaration's signing that would one day share the reverse side of the two-dollar bill from Jefferson's own face. Soon the pair were almost inseparable, taking almost daily excursions to tourist attractions and museums. (Jefferson's official duties as American Minister took up very little of his time.)

It remains unclear if Jefferson and Cosway became lovers in a physical sense, though their relationship was thick with romance and flirtatious declarations. Nothing in their voluminous correspondence—they continued to write one another until death—directly alludes to what would today be called "an affair." Yet Jefferson was famously guarded in such matters, and his relationship with Sally Hemings was also considered unlikely by most biographers until DNA tests proved it to be almost certain.

The romantic aspect of the relationship, whatever that may have been, appears to have ended with a start when Jefferson broke his wrist attempting to vault a fence in her company in September 1786. The injury was serious and ill-handled by the doctors. Jefferson wrote with his left hand for months, and never was able to play his beloved violin again. During his convalescence, Jefferson wrote Cosway a famous dialogue between his "head" and "heart," coyly reflecting on his internal dilemmas about their relationship.

But for a variety of reasons, the romance was always a doomed one. Cosway was a married woman, and a Roman Catholic to boot, meaning she could never obtain a divorce. Nor would Jefferson, who again was nurturing political hopes, necessarily have been willing to throw them away to marry a divorcee. Cosway could not imagine living in America; Jefferson could not imagine remaining in Europe. The two parted as friends, but no more.

Meanwhile, in 1787, Jefferson's eight-year-old daughter Polly had been sent to Paris to join her father. Accompanying her was James Hemings's teenage sister, Sally.

# Sally

Though the name "Sally Hemings" has dogged Jefferson's reputation from his presidency to the present day, surprisingly little is known about Hemings herself. This, clearly, is how

Jefferson wanted it. He makes no reference to Hemings in any of his correspondence beyond his general inventories of his property.

But today there is little doubt that Hemings was one of the most important people in his life, his lover and to some degree companion from 1787 until the end of his days. Hemings is known to have had six children, all of whom showed evidence of having a white father and bearing a striking physical resemblance to Jefferson. Jefferson was repeatedly accused in his lifetime of being their father. Their approximate conception dates all correspond with Jefferson's returns to Monticello. Hemings family oral history holds that Sally told her children that Jefferson was their father. Jefferson freed Hemings' family, including his purported children, in his will, but none of his other slaves.

Most conclusively, a DNA test of descendants of Sally's youngest son Eston showed that someone in the Jefferson male line was an ancestor. A few die-hard historians, generally of the far-right variety, continue to claim that one of Jefferson's brothers or nephews could have been the father of some or all of the children. While technically possible, no record exists of another male Jefferson visiting Monticello for all the dates required to have fathered the six children, nor was any other male Jefferson ever identified as a likely father until the DNA testing; previous efforts to exculpate Jefferson had usually focused on a son of his sister's named Peter Carr.

In light of the DNA evidence, historians have now generally accepted the Hemings family tradition that an affair between Jefferson and Sally Hemings began in Paris. Because slavery was illegal in mainland France, Sally was in an unusual position to bargain with the man who owned her, and she apparently struck a deal that she would return to America with Jefferson despite her chance at freedom, on the condition that he would free any children they had after his death. The situation was sordid on many levels—Sally was the teenage half-sister of Jefferson's dead wife, and any sexual relationship between a master and a slave is clearly bordering on rape—but it can at least be said for Jefferson that he kept this promise.

# Rebellion and the Constitution

Jefferson was overseas while the Articles of Confederation showed their increasing weakness. Missing out on these crucial years of the early republic created much of the gulf that would later separate his politics from those of the other Founding Fathers. In 1786, an anti-tax uprising turned violent in Western Massachusetts; this revolt—later called Shays's Rebellion for its leader, Daniel Shays—took the Confederation government more than six months to put down and was a crucial event in building support for a new constitution.

But from France, Jefferson saw the matter differently. He wrote to Madison that "no country should be long without [a rebellion]," and to another correspondent that "what signify a few lives lost in a century or two? The tree of liberty must from time to time be refreshed with the blood of patriots and tyrants. It is its natural manure." To Abigail Adams, he wrote "I like a little rebellion now and then. It is like a storm in the atmosphere."

To what degree Jefferson really believed all this is a matter of dispute. He tended to try on ideas and positions in his letters as other men might try on hats. Madison was used to this habit and often gently walked Jefferson back from his stupidest suggestions—at one point he talked Jefferson out of a proposal that all laws and debts expire once per generation so that the world could be created anew—but biographers often have not been so gracious.

Certainly Jefferson had no interest in "a little rebellion now and then" when he himself assumed the presidency, suppressing Burr's attempted uprising and protests against the embargo with all the force he could muster. What Jefferson really supported, unsurprisingly, was rebellion against his political opponents.

Still, Jefferson understood and mostly supported the move toward a stronger federal government. After all, his most frequent correspondent and closest political ally, James Madison, was spearheading the attempt. Jefferson's experience as a diplomat receiving orders from the disorganized Confederation government had shown him the need for the nation to have a stronger executive, at least for foreign affairs.

But Jefferson's distance from events allowed him to take a typically nuanced, arguably two-faced position. At one point, to Madison's frustration, he was encouraging some states to hold off ratification until a Bill of Rights could be passed. Jefferson's correspondence was so unclear, and his positions shifting so rapidly, that both Federalists and Anti-Federalists had publicly claimed him as a whole-hearted supporter. In the end, the Constitution was ratified without Jefferson having significantly affected the debate either way.

# Revolution

Meanwhile, the French political situation was rapidly deteriorating. Like England, France had gone massively into debt when the American Revolutionary War had expanded into a global conflict. Unlike England, France had no ready means to pay off this debt; the French people tended to see the military expenses as the crown's affair, rather than a problem for which the nation was responsible as a whole. Louis XVI appointed a succession of ministers who attempted to refashion France's financial system, but none could make serious progress in removing the privileges that exempted so many nobles from taxation, in part because the king failed to steadfastly support them and apply himself to the issue.

Ironically, just as the American Revolution started with wealthy citizens like John Hancock, Washington, and Jefferson rather than the "grass roots," the French Revolution's cries of "Tyrant!" first came from aristocrats in danger of losing their hereditary privileges. Soon Louis XVI was forced to call an Estates General, the first in 150 years. But at this meeting, the complaints of the "Third Estate"—the common people—soon overpowered those of the First Estate, the nobility. After an apparent failed attempt by Louis to lock them out of the Estates General, they declared themselves the National Assembly and the true representatives of the people in the famous "Tennis Court Oath."

Jefferson's loyalties in this situation were, of course, never in doubt. Lacking instructions from his government—the situation was developing too quickly for the rudimentary transatlantic communications of the day—Jefferson was forced to play a behind-the-scenes role in events, but he could not bring himself to stay out of them entirely. Most notably, he appears to have worked with the Marquis de Lafayette, a French former aide-de-camp of George Washington from the American Revolution, to help draft the Declaration of the Rights of Man and the Citizen of August 1789.

But at around this time, Jefferson received word that Congress had approved a requested leave of absence. He was leaving temporarily, he thought, fully intending to return to see what he assumed would be France's triumphant progression to a constitutional monarchy. But his country had need of him elsewhere now, and events in France would become far more complicated than anyone could have dreamed.

# Chapter 3:
# The Long Road to the Presidency

# Return

By the time Jefferson assumed the presidency in 1800, he had amassed a resume for the job almost unparalleled in American history. He had served as a state representative, a governor, a militia officer, a congressman (albeit to the Congress of the Confederation), an ambassador, Secretary of State, and vice president.

The next step in this chain was already waiting for him when he disembarked from France. He had hoped to stay only two and a half months in America before returning to Europe, but instead he learned the surprising news that the republic's first president under the new constitution, George Washington, had nominated him for Secretary of State. What was more, the Senate had already approved the appointment. Jefferson tried to decline the honor, but Washington insisted. The young country had few other experienced diplomats to fill the post—John Adams was now vice president, and Ben Franklin was in advanced old age—and Jefferson eventually accepted.

He passed a few months at Monticello, during which his daughter Patsy married Thomas Mann Randolph, Jr. Though Randolph would be politically successful, serving in the US House of Representatives and three terms as governor of Virginia, the marriage was a disaster. Randolph's alcoholism made Patsy's later life a misery, and she moved with her children to Boston to escape him.

In early 1790, Jefferson moved to New York, the temporary site of the national capital, and plunged back into the maelstrom of national politics.

# Hamilton

In New York, Jefferson met, apparently for the first time, the man who would be his nemesis for the next decade: Alexander Hamilton.

Hamilton was a self-made man in every way that Jefferson wished to be but was not. He was a Caribbean-born orphan who had displayed such prodigious talents that the wealthy men of his island had sent him to New York for a better education. Once there, Hamilton fell into revolutionary company and made a name for himself as Washington's chief aide throughout the war, as well as through personal heroism at the decisive battle of Yorktown. After the war, he became one of New York's most prominent lawyers as well as a leading advocate for the new US Constitution. Though many issues would later divide him from Madison, the two had partnered to write the Federalist Papers, a series of essays masterfully explaining the political theories behind the new Constitution and pressing for its passage. (John Jay also intended to contribute, but fell ill after completing only a few essays.)

Despite Hamilton's alliance with Madison, Jefferson saw much to be alarmed about in the younger man. Hamilton was an advocate of a strong executive, a position which he sometimes impoliticly referred to as a "monarch"; Jefferson had come to abhor the idea of even constitutional monarchy. As a New Yorker, Hamilton believed (correctly) that the nation's future lay in manufacturing and trade; as a Virginian, Jefferson believed (wrongly) that the nation's future lay in agriculture. (Much of the romanticization of the American farmer, including the subsidies that continue to make the agriculture industry a permanent welfare class, can be traced to Jefferson.) The economically astute Hamilton saw the necessity of banking and a stock market for a capitalist economy, including a national bank; the heavily indebted Jefferson believed that banks and stockbrokers were parasites and should not exist in a healthy society. Jefferson believed the greatest men who ever lived to be Isaac Newton, John Locke, and Francis Bacon. Hamilton hero-worshipped Julius Caesar, a choice that deeply alarmed politicians always worried that an American Caesar might try to wrest control of the fragile new government from the people.

Even the styles of the two men clashed. Born poor, Hamilton dressed rich and affected the manners of a gentleman. Born rich, Jefferson dressed poor and insisted on dispensing with protocol. He even caused several diplomatic incidents during his presidency by insisting on receiving foreign ministers in his dressing gown and slippers, for example, or failing to seat their wives properly at dinner.

Like many of his generation, Jefferson was congenitally unable to recognize that legitimate disagreement in government was possible, or that there could be such a thing as a loyal opposition. In his philosophy, there was a popular will, singular and united. Since he and his allies sought to implement this will, anyone who opposed them was opposing the people. Anyone who opposed the people was by definition a secret monarchist and a supporter of tyranny.

In Jefferson's presidency, this unshakeable sense of self-righteousness would deafen him to protests against his foolish embargo, and do much to worsen the divisions in the nation. But for now, it merely divided Washington's cabinet. In Jefferson's paranoid politics, Hamilton was not merely an opponent; he was the leader of a cabal bent on destroying American democracy from the inside out and returning the country to monarchy or dictatorship. Jefferson soon found himself locked in battle with Hamilton on almost every issue. The first of these was the national debt.

# The Dinner Table Bargain

Hamilton's most audacious plan for the new federal government was that it should assume the debts each state had incurred during the war. Many of these debts were to foreign countries, and the outstanding debts were a major headache for American negotiators who represented the federal government but had no power to compel the states. Hamilton also saw the voluntary assumption of debt by the federal government as a subtle way to establish its supremacy: the states would be reliant on the federal power that now paid off their debts, and the individuals and governments that had financed the loans would now have a sense of investment in the federal government's survival.

Unlike later Hamiltonian plans, Jefferson had some sympathy for this view. He had long urged that the US settle its outstanding debts to his beloved France, and had seen firsthand how the state debts hamstrung American diplomats. But wealthy Virginia had already settled its debt, as had several other Southern states. Such states understandably perceived Hamilton's plan as penalizing them for having promptly settled their own debts, as they would now be forced to pay an equal share of the national debt regardless. Hamilton's plan therefore stalled in the House of Representatives.

Jefferson invited Hamilton and Madison to dine with him on June 20, 1790, to discuss the issue. Madison was now serving in the House of Representatives, where he was arguably the most prominent member. Like Jefferson, Madison seems to have been wary of Hamilton's plan but not totally opposed. Still, he sensed an opportunity for Virginia to gain significantly.

Over dinner that night, the three men (or in Jefferson's unlikely retelling, the other two men only, as Jefferson merely watched) struck the most famous backroom deal of the early republic, the Dinner Table Bargain. Jefferson and Madison agreed that while they could not publicly support Hamilton's plan—it would have been political suicide for them to do so—

they would not organize opposition to it, allowing it to pass Congress.

In exchange, Hamilton agreed to support moving the national capital from his native New York to the Potomac River on land currently part of Virginia. The move would increase the South's prestige, and Jefferson—always warning of the corruption of cities, Paris apparently excluded—believed that only a rural site would allow the government to remain virtuous. The three also worked out a formula for Virginia's debt to be adjusted to make the new debt arrangement more palatable.

Both factions emerged able to claim some sort of victory, but future disputes would not be so civil.

# The First Bank of the United States

In 1791, Hamilton began to push for a national bank. He correctly understood that Britain's financial structure was a key element in its global supremacy. Whereas the growing cost of worldwide wars drove a country like France to collapse, Britain was able to manage the debt through its Bank of England. Such a bank would also be able to manage US currency, avoiding the horrific inflation that had made the Confederation's dollars almost worthless. Though this institution is called the Federal Reserve today, essentially Hamilton was proposing what has come to be seen as a vital pillar of national finance.

To Jefferson, however, this proposal was an abomination. He was offended on principle by the idea of modeling any facet of government on the British model, but more importantly, he believed that having so much money under government control would lead inevitably to corruption. He further feared that it would greatly empower bankers and special interests at the expense of farmers, undermining republican virtue, and strengthen the federal government, allowing it to oppress the people. Finally, he opposed the exercise of any power by the federal government not explicitly granted under the Constitution.

From a historical perspective, this last argument was the most interesting. Only three years into the new government, one of the great fault lines of American politics had already emerged: "strict constructionism" versus "broad constructionism." The former view, advocated to President Washington by Jefferson and Madison, held that the federal government must request a Constitutional amendment to exercise any power not already named. (Jefferson himself later found as president that exceptions were necessary. Though some in his party felt a Constitutional amendment would be necessary to make the Louisiana Purchase, Jefferson refused to risk the opportunity for this legal technicality and simply assumed the power to make the purchase.)

The broad constructionist view, advocated by Hamilton, focused on the clause that allowed Congress to take all "necessary and proper" actions to carry out its duties. The Bank of the United States would help Congress fulfill several of its duties, and therefore could be formed as long as the Constitution did not explicitly forbid it.

Washington inclined to Hamilton's view, and after Congress passed the bank bill, he signed it into law. Jefferson was appalled. He would never quite work out where Washington sat in his binary view of the world—on the side of virtue and democracy or on the side of the oppressors—but in incidents like this preferred to see Washington as a good man misled by bad counselors. From this day on, he and Madison began to organize against Hamilton from behind the scenes. America's first two-party system was coming into being.

## The Whiskey Rebellion

Another part of Hamilton's financial plan was an excise tax on liquor to pay off the national debt. This provision was rejected by Congress when he first proposed it, but later accepted when it became clear the federal government was in desperate need of money.

The tax was unpopular in rural areas, where liquors such as corn whiskey proved a reliable way for farmers to use, store, and transport surplus grain. Protests began in 1791 and became increasingly violent, particularly in Western Pennsylvania. These events would come to a head in 1794, when Washington himself led an army into the field to subdue the protestors, the only time a sitting US president has led troops into combat. No protestors were willing to fight the legendary Washington, of course, and the "Whiskey Rebellion" melted away without a shot being fired.

For Washington, Hamilton, Adams, and other "Federalists," the incident was a satisfying contrast to Shays's Rebellion, which had paralyzed the Confederation government and led to the Constitutional Convention. But to Jefferson, Madison, and their growing faction, the suppression of the "rebellion" was one more example of Hamilton's pernicious influence and tendencies to tyranny.

Jefferson was reduced to complaining about the incident from afar, however, for by this point, he had already left Washington's cabinet.

## Resignation

Jefferson's strenuous opposition to Washington's signing of the bank bill had created a serious rift between the two men, but in these days before political parties were an acknowledged reality, neither man knew how to handle it. Washington considered dismissing Jefferson, as any modern president would do, but on reflection kept him in his post. Though he leaned toward what would later be called the Federalist Party,

Washington believed that national unity was the paramount concern, and he exerted himself in the increasingly difficult task of keeping all the emerging factions unified behind him. (Also showing his allegiance to the mostly northern Federalist party, Washington mentioned to a friend that if the Union should dissolve within his lifetime, he intended to move north and side with those states against his native Virginia.) Jefferson still held hope for Washington, however, and in 1792 urged him to run for re-election to uphold the principles that would later be called Jeffersonian democracy. Washington ran for re-election and won handily, of course, but he was no closer to Jefferson's views than before.

Meanwhile, Jefferson hired a newspaper editor named Philip Freneau to wage war against Hamilton by press and pamphlet. Hamilton responded in kind, attacking Jefferson's faction both anonymously and under his own name. Jefferson complained to Madison that the prolific Hamilton was "a host unto himself" in these escalating written battles.

In Washington's second term, foreign policy became the primary concern. As the wars of the French Revolutionary government escalated in Europe, American shipping was under attack by both sides. Neutrality of American vessels during European conflicts would help start more than a few of the country's wars, but for now Washington was determined that the country not be embroiled in another conflict so soon after the bloodshed and disruption of the Revolution.

In 1793, the French Revolutionary government sent the divisive Edmond-Charles Genêt as ambassador to rally American support for their cause, and partisanship sharpened on both sides of the divide. Jefferson and Madison celebrated Genêt as a kindred spirit from a kindred people, feting him at dinners and rallies. Meanwhile, Adams, Hamilton, and others of their faction abhorred the violence and executions of the French Revolution, which by now had been disavowed even by the Marquis de Lafayette, and sought to ally with the more stable British.

After much deliberation, Washington sided with the Federalists. Genêt had done his cause more harm than good by openly calling on the American people to defy, or even overthrow, Washington to ally with the French. Jefferson was aware of these doings and at times tacitly encouraged them, while remaining in Washington's cabinet and baldly lying to him about Genêt's actions. At last even Jefferson realized that Genêt was a hopeless political liability, but the damage was done. (Genêt was muzzled the following year when the Jacobins began the Reign of Terror and politely requested his return to answer a few questions; Genêt wisely declined, and spent his remaining years in America, marrying a daughter of Jefferson's future vice president, George Clinton.)

Increasingly unable to play both sides against one another without exposure, Jefferson abruptly quit the cabinet. Washington was outraged and never spoke to him again. Jefferson swore that he would have no further role in politics, but few observers were convinced this time. As John Adams wryly observed to his wife, "It is marvelous how political plants grow in the shade."

# Party Boss

So Jefferson again returned to Monticello, where he was always happiest. But he continued his subscriptions to newspapers this time—the early years of the American Republic were a golden age for cheap mass journalism—and Madison, Monroe, and others carefully kept him abreast of the rapidly developing national situation.

From Monticello, Jefferson coordinated the creation of America's first real political party while steadfastly insisting that political parties were one of the great evils of democracy. (Indeed, at the time, "democracy" itself was considered a dirty word, signifying mob rule as opposed to the reasoned deliberations of a republic's elite representatives.) Washington's suppression of the Whiskey Rebellion became an important talking point, but nothing could compare to the Jay Treaty.

Negotiated in 1795 by Chief Justice John Jay, the treaty pledged peace and favorable trade terms with Britain at the expense of Revolutionary France. From the standpoint of history, Washington's decision was a wise one. He had correctly bet on which country would remain dominant on the world stage, and he had postponed a foreign war until his country would be more stable. But with the violence of the redcoats still a living memory for most Americans—the war was just a little more than a decade in the past—Jay's Treaty was highly controversial.

Jefferson and Madison saw their moment to strike, organizing opposition in every state. Mass rallies were held to protest the treaty, the government was deluged with letters, and graffiti appeared such as "Damn John Jay! Damn everyone who won't damn John Jay!! Damn everyone that won't put lights in his windows and sit up all night damning John Jay!!!" Democratic-Republican newspaper editors called Jay an "arch-traitor" and called for his torture and murder. Jay joked that he could safely ride by night the entire length of New England by the light of the bonfires burning his effigies.

But Washington threw his full prestige behind the treaty, and Hamilton and his allies were active in the press as well. In the end, the Senate ratified Jay's Treaty by exactly the required two-thirds majority. Jefferson and Madison were disappointed to have lost their struggle, but they had laid the groundwork for another important prize: the election of 1796.

# Jefferson for President

In September 1796, Washington surprised both his cabinet and the nation with the announcement that he would not seek a third term as president. Though he was assured re-election, he had tired of the hurly-burly of politics and wished to set the precedent that men would not hold the presidency until their deaths. (No one at the time, certainly not Washington, seriously imagined the possibility of a female president.)

Both factions launched into action. The political culture of the day demanded that candidates seem disinterested in public office, under the belief that any man who actively sought power was unworthy to hold it. This was, of course, a pose; both Jefferson and sitting Vice President John Adams, the two most likely candidates, were both desperate to be president. But custom demanded that they do battle through surrogates rather than taking to the hustings themselves.

The Democratic-Republican press attacked Adams along the usual lines that he was a "monocrat" or monarchist, and a lackey of the British. Jefferson in turn was lambasted as an atheist—not quite true, though certainly most Americans would have been shocked by his real beliefs. With similar half-truth, Federalist pamphlets called him an unabashed Francophile who would put that nation's interests over his own country.

The Electoral College decided narrowly for Adams, 71 to 68. But under the rules of the day—later amended in Jefferson's own presidency—the man with the second-most votes became the vice president. For the second time, therefore, Jefferson would have a key role in a Federalist-leaning administration. Meanwhile, Jefferson's running mate, the amoral New York politician Aaron Burr, was angered that southern Democratic-Republicans had refused to vote for him as promised in the Electoral College, where he garnered only 30 votes. Burr's grudge would one day nearly cost Jefferson the presidency.

## Vice President

Even today, the vice presidency is a widely ridiculed office with almost no power. In the early years of the republic, the vice president did even less. John Adams had tried to take an active role in presiding over the Senate, but Jefferson was passive even in this respect. Preferring writing to speaking as usual, however, he did draft an influential Manual of Parliamentary Practice to guide Congressional debate.

Jefferson mostly spent the four years of his vice presidency trying to undermine the administration of which he was nominally a part. The greatest issue of the Adams years was the so-called "Quasi-War" with France, in which French privateers preyed on American shipping without war ever quite being declared. Jefferson made no secret that his loyalties were with the French and against Adams. To modern eyes, his actions appear at times to verge on outright treason. Yet in Jefferson's mind, it was Adams who was acting against the American people's interests and wishes. Siding with a foreign power against the US president could be justified if that president was a secret monarchist. Consequently, when Adams sent representatives to France to negotiate for peace, Jefferson sent instructions of his own to the French government to stall and sabotage the talks. No presidential candidate would again so blatantly undermine the peace talks of a sitting president until Richard Nixon's apparent sabotage of Lyndon Johnson's Vietnam negotiations.

Jefferson's scheming continued to backfire on him, however. In early 1797, he wrote to an Italian correspondent about "men who were Samsons in the field... who have had their heads shorn by the harlot England." The reference to Washington was clear, and when Jefferson's correspondent published the letter in Italy, American Federalists had a field day reprinting it for their readers, accusing Jefferson of betraying his political patron and America's most respected figure.

## The XYZ Affair

In 1798, when Adams's negotiations with France failed, Jefferson demanded through surrogates that a full record of the talks be made public. Rather than showing Adams to have been insincere, as Jefferson hoped, the record not only proved the sincerity of Adams's attempt at peace, but that the American negotiators had been turned away when unwilling to pay the bribes of corrupt French officials (named as X, Y, and Z in the papers).

The so-called "XYZ Affair" enraged the American public and brought the nation to the brink of war. One Federalist declared, "Millions for defense, not one penny for tribute." Adams asked for and received a massive expansion to both the American army and navy. More controversially, he also signed the Alien and Sedition Acts into law, giving the federal government new powers to detain suspicious foreigners as well as administration critics. Though the law only authorized the jailing of journalists who printed falsehoods, the statute was vague enough to guarantee that it would be abused for partisan reasons.

All this was the stuff of Jefferson's nightmares. Adams was now at the head of a growing military, riding a popular wave toward war with the world's only other democratic power. Democratic-Republican newspaper editors were being jailed by overzealous Federalist authorities. Jefferson's bogeyman, Hamilton, appeared likely to take charge of the army.

But as always, Jefferson refused to see that Adams's intentions were admirable. Even as Jefferson accused him of warmongering, Adams defied popular opinion and his own party to attempt one more round of peace talks with France. These were successful, and war was averted—though word reached America just too late to help him re-election in

1800. Amazingly, Jefferson maintained to the end of his life that Adams had craftily tried to instigate a war with France, and only the popular movement of the Democratic-Republicans had stopped him. He simply could not admit that his friend might have been the more honest of the two after all.

# Kentucky and Virginia Resolutions

Jefferson and Madison were sufficiently alarmed by the Alien and Sedition Acts that they proposed an extreme step. In 1798, Jefferson drafted a resolution that was then passed by the legislature of the new states of Kentucky, declaring that states had the power to "nullify" federal laws that were unconstitutional. Madison wrote and passed a milder version in Virginia—an ironic reversal for a man who had once advocated that the federal government should be allowed to veto state laws.

Though it raised alarm around the country, their doctrine had little impact at the time. The election of 1800 would replace Adams with Jefferson, and the issues became moot. But by trying to make state governments the final arbiter of the US Constitution, Jefferson and Madison unintentionally set the nation on a course toward tremendous bloodshed. Hamilton biographer Ron Chernow has written that "the theoretical damage of the Kentucky and Virginia Resolutions was deep and lasting, and was a recipe for disunion," setting the stage for the American Civil War. George Washington himself feared that if this doctrine was "systematically and pertinaciously pursued," it would "dissolve the union or produce coercion."

# The Adams-Jefferson Rematch

Adams's popularity had peaked during the XYZ Affair, and had he chosen to go to war at that moment, his re-election would probably have been assured. But he chose the more difficult road of peace and could no longer count on reflexive wartime support.

A series of unforced errors by Federalists further helped the Democratic-Republican cause. The editors jailed under the Alien-Sedition Acts, though few in number, had become a cause célèbre in the Democratic-Republican press, convincing many of Jefferson's otherwise ludicrous charge that Adams sought to make himself a king.

The irascible, undiplomatic Adams was also having trouble holding the Federalist coalition together. He had unwisely kept on Washington's entire cabinet, rather than appointing his own people, and many of them were more loyal to Hamilton than to him. The equally temperamental Hamilton was enraged with Adams for failing to go to war, and Adams finally fired most of the cabinet in the same year he was seeking re-election. Hamilton retaliated by releasing a pamphlet blasting Adams as unfit for office and borderline insane. (He carefully noted that this still made Adams better than Jefferson, but readers could not have been greatly reassured by this qualification.) Even as the Federalist Party was disintegrating—it would in fact never elect another president—its attack dogs continued to circulate the same old charges against Jefferson, but now with far less effectiveness.

In this era of poor communications, the results came in gradually. It slowly became clear that the Democratic-Republicans had indeed defeated John Adams, but there was an unexpected twist. Seeking to avoid a repeat of Burr's 1796 embarrassment, all its electors had been instructed to cast votes both for Jefferson and Burr. The strategy worked perfectly: Jefferson and Burr received an equal number of votes. But with no distinction between presidential and vice-presidential votes, this meant that the two men were now tied for the presidency. The election was then left to the US House of Representatives to decide.

## Jefferson vs. Burr

Suddenly finding himself in reach of America's highest office, the roguish Burr was in no hurry to step aside. Nor was the Federalist-controlled House in any hurry to certify Jefferson's results. The will of the people had been clear; the Democratic-Republicans had selected Jefferson as their man, and the electors had voted accordingly. Yet many Federalists wondered if Burr, a New Yorker with deep ties in commerce, might be better than the man they had portrayed for years as the godless apostle of France and anarchy. Today, we would be outraged at the suggestion that the popular will be rejected by the Electoral College or Congress, but the Electoral College had been created by the Founding Fathers for exactly that purpose: to overturn the popular will if the elected representatives found it wisest to do so.

The controversy dragged on for ballot after ballot as the country grew increasingly nervous. Democratic-Republicans began to mutter darkly about revolt and civil war if the Federalists cheated Jefferson of the presidency. The tie was broken with help from an unlikely source: Alexander Hamilton, who despised Jefferson but nonetheless realized that the unprincipled Burr was a far greater danger to the nation. After Hamilton's lobbying and some last-minute deals by Jefferson about retaining Federalist appointees and naval expenditures, enough Federalist representatives were persuaded to cast blank ballots that Jefferson's supporters carried the day.

Despite the unexpected dispute over the final results, Jefferson assumed the presidency on schedule—the first peaceful, democratic transition between opposition parties in living memory. It was a landmark in world history, far more important than Washington's succession by Adams, and both Federalist and Democratic-Republicans were aware of it. Adams declined to see his successor the week of the inauguration, and relations between the two former friends would take decades to recover. But both men deserve credit for the larger accomplishment, which set the precedent for centuries of nonviolent American power-sharing.

# Chapter 4: The Glorious First Term

# Inauguration

From the beginning, Jefferson was determined to set a contrast between his own style and that of his predecessors. With no precedents to follow, Washington had maintained some of the trappings of a European monarch, such as being addressed as "Your Excellency." Adams had ridden to his inauguration in a massive carriage. Jefferson wore a plain suit, refused to wear a ceremonial sword, and proceeded to his own inauguration on foot, arriving with mud on his pants and boots. After he was sworn in, there would be neither balls nor feasts. He would sell the president's coach and many White House furnishings, and make himself available to any White House visitor, no matter how lowly. (As a new, planned city in the wilderness with less than ten thousand permanent residents, Washington, D.C. was still remote and rural enough to make such a policy possible.)

Jefferson was always a terrible speaker, even by the low standards of the bookish Founding Fathers, and his inaugural address was almost inaudible to his listeners. But its content was magnificent, inspiring to Democratic-Republicans and reassuring to Federalists. He struck the expected notes of calling for a restoration of individual liberties and a reduction in the federal government. But he also reached out to his political opponents in what would become the speech's most famous passage: "every difference of opinion is not a difference of principle. We have called by different names brethren of the same principle. We are all Republicans, we are all Federalists." This was a very different tune from Democratic-Republican campaign propaganda, which had painted Federalists as just short of traitors, but Jefferson would be far from the last new president to call for unity once it was clear that he would be at the head of things.

## Cabinet

For his cabinet, Jefferson appointed his right-hand man Madison as Secretary of State. In this period, this office was generally seen as the most direct route to the presidency, whereas the vice presidency was held by lesser figures like George Clinton, Elbridge Gerry, or Daniel D. Tompkins, whose names will be barely recognizable to the casual student of history. (The United States was singularly lucky not to lose a sitting head of state to death until William Henry Harrison's passing in 1841.)

Jefferson appointed the brilliant Swiss immigrant Albert Gallatin as his Secretary of the Treasury. Gallatin was charged with reducing the national debt and dismantling every possible vestige of Hamilton's financial system, which by now had had a decade to entrench itself. His other three cabinet appointments proved capable but less distinguished: Levi Lincoln as Attorney General, Henry Dearborn as Secretary of War, and Benjamin Stoddert as Secretary of the Navy.

For lesser offices, Jefferson sought to appoint a wider range of men than the Federalists had selected, rather than restricting his appointments to the elites. But as biographer R. B. Bernstein observes, Jefferson's choices were still shaped by some prejudices of the day. Secretary Gallatin made the groundbreaking suggestion of appointing women to some offices in 1807, but Jefferson rejected him out of hand: "The appointment of a woman to office is an innovation for which the public is not prepared, nor am I."

# Debt

Jefferson's top priorities as president were to pay off as much of Hamilton's federal debt as possible and begin reducing the size of the government. As Gordon Wood points out in Empire of Liberty, the federal government was already miniscule by today's standards; Secretary of State Madison, for example, had a staff of eight, and the War Department was run by only seventeen people, including Secretary Dearborn himself. Jefferson nonetheless set out to reduce things even further. He cut offices, slashed budgets, and halted Adams's naval building program. Overall, he reduced military expenditures by more than 50%, citing Napoleon Bonaparte's recent assumption of power in France as a warning that standing armies spelled doom for republican governments.

Jefferson and his Democratic-Republican allies in Congress were correspondingly able to abolish many of Hamilton's direct taxes, reducing the federal presence in the lives of ordinary citizens. In rebudgeting, Jefferson benefited from favorable economic conditions for which he was glad to take the credit. Again, Wood says it best: "For most citizens the federal presence was reduced to the delivery of the mail." In eight years as president, Jefferson successfully reduced the federal debt from $83 million to $57 million, a reduction of almost one-third.

The Bank of the United States proved more durable. Gallatin was wiser about banking than his chief, and eventually persuaded Jefferson that the institution must be kept. But its role was increasingly reduced during the Jefferson years, and its powers assumed by the state banks. (Democratic-Republicans in Congress would eventually abolish it without presidential action in 1811, two years after Jefferson left office.) Since the national bank issued no paper currency, this proved to be a blessing in disguise; the state banks quickly circulated paper notes of their own, allowing the necessary inflation for the economy to expand.

One last financial issue that bedeviled Jefferson was the question of patronage. When he assumed office, the government was staffed almost entirely with Federalists, as no other party had ever held office. Jefferson held an idealistic, meritocratic view of how new candidates should be chosen, but few in his party shared his purity. He was repeatedly caught between the political necessity of pleasing allies on the one hand and the desire to appear nonpartisan and meritocratic on the other. Though the "civil service" question would not bother Jefferson's immediate successors—there would be no change of party again until Andrew Jackson succeeded John Quincy Adams in 1829—this dilemma would continue to trouble 19th-century politics, and even become a major issue in Reconstruction Era presidential campaigns.

# Undoing Adams: The Callender Pardon

Jefferson also sought to undo what he saw as some of the worst excesses of his predecessor, John Adams. He pardoned those imprisoned under the Alien and Sedition Acts, which were then repealed by his Congressional allies. One of these men, James T. Callender, was a vicious pamphleteer whom Jefferson had secretly encouraged and financially supported for years. Callender felt that Jefferson now owed him more than a mere pardon, and demanded to be made a postmaster in Virginia. Jefferson refused.

Embittered, Callender then joined the Federalist press, attacking Jefferson with the same viciousness that he once had Adams. In one of his diatribes, he revealed that Jefferson had secretly employed him during the previous campaigns. When Jefferson unwisely attempted to deny this, Callender produced Jefferson's letters and proved him a liar. Callender was also the first to publicize the Sally Hemings allegations, running a series of stories exposing the relationship. Jefferson maintained a studied silence on the issue throughout his life, never confirming or denying his parentage of Hemings's children.

# Undoing Adams: The "Midnight Judges"

After losing the presidential election but before leaving office, John Adams made a series of federal judicial appointments, including a new Chief Justice of the Supreme Court, John Marshall. With this appointment, Adams reshaped the course of US history, though none could fully appreciate it at the time. Outraged Democratic-Republicans called the appointments the "Midnight Judges," claiming that Adams had stayed up late into the night the day before he left office making appointments to stack the benches with Federalists. (In reality, Adams appointed them over several weeks.)

Jefferson dealt with most of Adams's lame-duck appointments by simply asking his Congressional allies to reduce the size of the federal judiciary, as he did so many other departments. Rather than removing individual judges from office, they abolished the offices themselves. But Marshall, who could not be so easily done away with, proved a thorn in Jefferson's side for the next eight years. Though a fellow Virginian, and a cousin of Jefferson's to boot, Marshall was a Federalist who believed in a strong government and had been a leading advocate for the new US Constitution. Politicians of the Federalist Party never again mounted a significant challenge to Jefferson after Hamilton tore apart the party in 1800, but Marshall remained on the bench to provide important checks on Jefferson's increasingly imperial instincts.

# An Independent Judiciary

One of the most crucial Supreme Court cases in US history—the one that made all the others possible—came three years into Jefferson's presidency. The issue at stake was a petty one: a "Midnight Judge" appointee named William Marbury had been denied his post by Secretary of State James Madison. But the Court's ruling, penned by Marshall, was a work of legal genius with lasting implications.

Several questions were put before the Court, including if Marbury had been unlawfully denied his office and if the Supreme Court even had jurisdiction to overrule actions of the executive branch. Marshall cunningly refused to answer the questions in the proper order. The Supreme Court did indeed have jurisdiction, Marshall ruled, but Madison had acted within his rights and Marbury had no remedy. The resulting decision was the ultimate Pyrrhic victory for the Democratic-Republicans. Technically, they had won the case, and a direct clash between the executive and judicial branches was avoided for now. But Marshall had asserted the fundamental supremacy of the judiciary, a doctrine known later as "judicial review."

This doctrine proved to be a mixed blessing for later generations. No other modern country gives its courts such sweeping power to settle its society's most controversial issues, including slavery, the death penalty, abortion, civil rights, gay marriage, campaign finance reform, health-care reform, environmental legislation, and immigration law. Yet it also allowed a final authority for political disputes unresolvable in the regular system, such as the disputed Bush-Gore election of 2000 or Richard Nixon's attempt to withhold the tape recordings on which he obstructed justice. For better or for worse, this doctrine was the Marshall court's gift to America.

In 1804, Democratic-Republicans took one last swing at the Court's Federalists. At the time, the Supreme Court justices rode the circuit, presiding over individual federal trials, as well as meeting as a full court. Justice Samuel Chase had become known for issuing lengthy "instructions" from the bench that were in fact harangues against Democratic-Republican politicians. With a good deal of encouragement from Jefferson, Congressional Democratic-Republicans brought impeachment charges against Chase for allowing his political bias to affect his actions, and hoped to target Marshall next. But though the House impeached him, the Senate refused to convict, with a majority of senators arguing that impeachment should be reserved for actual violations of the law or failure to perform the duties of the office. No Supreme Court justice has been impeached since (though Lyndon Johnson appointee Abe Fortas came close for his ethics violations in 1968). The independence of the judicial branch was secure.

## Jefferson at War

Surprisingly for a man who so feared the role of military power in a democracy, President Jefferson initiated America's first foreign war. Adams had fought the "Quasi-War" with France, of course, but as we have seen, he did everything in his power to prevent an escalation to full-scale war; the result was a series of half-hearted naval engagements that killed a few dozen sailors and marines on each side. But when Jefferson assumed office, he still had the Federalists' new-built navy at his disposal, and he knew just what to do with it.

Today the Horn of Africa is notorious for the pirate gangs that prey on international shipping lanes. The equivalent in Jefferson's day was the "Barbary Coast," a now-outdated term for North Africa. The Barbary States were essentially extortion rackets the size of city-states, which thrived on the tribute paid by nations that did not want their ships hijacked, and the booty taken from the ships that failed to pay this tribute. Even great powers like Britain and France paid this tribute. Presidents Washington and Adams had both followed suit, paying tribute as well as ransoms for captured Americans. One treaty with the Barbary State of Tripoli even sought to appease the Muslim rulers by pledging that the US was "not, in any sense, founded on the Christian religion."

Ironically for a man who would nearly destroy his country with an embargo, Jefferson was a staunch believer in free trade as a fundamental human right. Not only were the Barbary States despotisms within their borders, they were also interfering with the commerce of other free peoples. In 1807, Jefferson's attempt to pick a similar fight with the British and French would have disastrous results, but subduing the Barbary States was a far more achievable goal. He had long urged Washington and then Adams to make war against them; when he assumed the presidency himself, he finally had his own chance to take action.

## Victory

The Barbary State of Tripoli quickly gave him an excuse; displeased by not receiving as much tribute as Algiers, Pasha Yusuf ibn Ali Karamanli ordered the flag of the American consulate in Tripoli cut down. Seeing his opportunity, Jefferson dispatched a squadron of ships to attack Tripoli's fleet in 1801. The US commanders were cautious, even lethargic in their pursuit of Tripoli's fleet, and little happened for the next two years. But in 1803, the USS Philadelphia was caught on a sandbar and captured by Tripoli's pirates. Pasha Yusuf demanded a $3 million ransom for their return, what was then about a twentieth of the entire US national debt; an equivalent portion of the federal budget today would be $950 billion.

Jefferson's response was swift and decisive. He dispatched more ships, and authorized US Consul William Eaton to lead a squad of marines overland to depose Pasha Yusuf. All of these plans worked better than anyone had a right to expect. A squadron of marines led by Stephen Decatur slipped into Tripoli's harbor to burn the captured Philadelphia, and escaped without losing a single man. Even famed British naval commander Horatio Lord Nelson called it "the most bold and daring act of the age," and Decatur became an overnight celebrity, the namesake of towns and counties across America. Meanwhile, US naval squadrons forced other Barbary States to abandon their support of Tripoli. Isolated, blockaded, and fearing overthrow by Eaton's forces, who had now allied with the pasha's exiled brother, Yusuf sued for peace in 1805.

The import of Jefferson's victory was more psychological than practical. The other Barbary States continued to prey on shipping, and the US would pay tribute again in the future. The US even still paid $600,000 for the release of the Philadelphia's crew. Eaton was deeply embittered by Jefferson's failure to see through what we would today call "regime change," and would later be recruited into Burr's ludicrous military escapades.

But it was nonetheless a formative event for US foreign policy, the first of many overseas "police actions." The American people could celebrate victory in their first foreign war, and they began to see their nation's quest for freedom not only as a domestic ideal, but one that could be exported to other corners of the world. They had done what the European great powers had not and subdued a minor threat to world commerce. The war would be immortalized in the first line of the "Marines' Hymn," the official hymn of the US Marine Corps: "From the Halls of Montezuma to the shores of Tripoli..."

# Haiti

One problem that demanded Jefferson's attention throughout his presidency was the question of Haiti. As difficult as it is to picture today, when Haiti is often a byword for poverty and desperation, the Haiti of the late eighteenth century was the crown jewel of France's overseas possessions, a source of incredible wealth thanks to its large sugar plantations. But these plantations were worked by slaves, and in 1791, the slaves revolted.

Mainland France was still roiling with the chaos of revolution, and many of the French Revolution's ideals of human equality had trickled down to the enslaved people of Haiti, building pressure for revolution there as well. What followed was the largest slave uprising in world history and a decade and a half of bloody, disorganized fighting. The factions split along racial, class, and geographical lines, and men, women, and children of every group were at times massacred.

Black leader Toussaint Louverture managed to maintain some semblance of control at the beginning of Jefferson's presidency, but the new French emperor, Napoleon Bonaparte—a Corsican artillery officer who had seized control of France after the failure of the revolutionary experiment—captured him after a false offer to negotiate. Napoleon attempted to subdue the island and reclaim it for France, but his troops were devastated by yellow fever and retreated ignominiously.

Jefferson's own loyalties were torn. The people of Haiti were manifestly fighting for freedom against a tyrant, yet slaves rising up against their masters was the stuff of Jefferson's nightmares. He and the Democratic-Republicans therefore maintained a policy of studied neutrality throughout the conflict, which ultimately benefited the revolutionaries, who needed foreign imports of arms and war material far more than the French. But in 1804, new Haitian emperor Jean-Jacques Dessalines arranged the massacre of the island's remaining white population, approximately 4,000 people. This genocide sealed the hostility of southern Americans (and many northerners as well) to the new Haitian regime. Even after the nation returned to democratic rule, the US refused to formally acknowledge the existence of the hemisphere's only other republic until the Southern states seceded from the Union in the Civil War.

For Jefferson personally, the massacres forever fixed his belief that whites and blacks could not live together in peace. No matter how unjust, slavery must continue for the present to prevent similar bloodshed on American soil.

# Louisiana Purchase

Nothing Jefferson did, not even his famous preamble to the Declaration of Independence, shaped the nation so much as the Louisiana Purchase. Only James K. Polk's Mexican-American War would reshape the boundaries of the country so radically. Ironically, the purchase was unplanned, perhaps the most consequential "impulse buy" in world history. But Jefferson saw his opportunity and seized it with characteristic energy.

The United States has always been blessed with weak neighbors. Canada was sparsely populated and its long border indefensible, making it impractical for the British to consider using it to attack. France had been driven from the continent in the Seven Years' War, and even its most prized Caribbean possession had been lost to a slave revolt. Only

Spain still controlled large parts of what would later be the continental United States, and Spain was widely and correctly regarded as a crumbling empire that had been in steady decline since the sixteenth-century golden age of King Philip II. Americans could be confident that when their line of expansion began to abut the Spanish, these territories would fall into their laps.

But in the Napoleonic Wars, Spain's territories suddenly fell under the control of France once again. In 1802, Napoleon set off alarm bells across the country when he announced new duties on all American goods passing through the port of New Orleans; since this city controlled the mouth of the Mississippi River, Americans in the growing Midwest had no other outlets for their goods. If they could not reopen this port, Jefferson told one confidant, the US must "marry ourselves to the British fleet and nation." Given Jefferson's long-time Anglophobia, it was a shocking statement, one that revealed the depth of his desperation.

First, though, he intended to reach out to Napoleon directly. Jefferson dispatched Robert Livingston--a diplomat who had served with him on the committee that wrote the Declaration of Independence—and James Monroe to France to negotiate the purchase of New Orleans. To Livingston and Monroe's astonishment, Napoleon offered them the chance to purchase not merely New Orleans, but the entire Western United States. The disaster in Haiti had led him to fear that any other French armies sent to the New World would be similarly swallowed up by disease, and Napoleon did not believe his American territories would be defensible in case of war. What was more, he desperately needed funds to resume war with England. Later, Napoleon would consider the sale one of his greatest mistakes, but for now, he was game.

It was lucky that Jefferson had dispatched Monroe as his agent; Monroe was close enough with both Jefferson and Madison that he could confidently exceed his orders and purchase all of the Louisiana Territory, not merely New Orleans. In the end, Monroe and Livingston negotiated the purchase of 900,000 square miles for $15 million, about three cents an acre. When he received word of the deal, Jefferson was flabbergasted at their good fortune. America's borders would again be clear of serious threats, and the land would provide enough space for many generations of virtuous republican farmers.

But with typical partisan churlishness, the Federalists moved to block him. They feared the expansion of the Southern slave power into this new territory. Some of Jefferson's own party also hesitated over this treaty, as the Constitution had not explicitly granted the federal government the power to purchase new lands. Jefferson was now hoisted on the petard of his own strict constructionism. He considered seeking a constitutional amendment, but hearing that Napoleon was already reconsidering the sale, he decided that there was no time for the lengthy process of ratification by the states. The purchase was ultimately approved by Congress by only the thinnest of margins. Spain attempted to protest that France was not the rightful owner of this territory and therefore could not sell it, but a bit of saber-rattling along the border of Florida—still a Spanish possession, though not for much longer—was all it took to quiet the enfeebled power.

# Consequences of the Purchase

The Purchase was a triumph on a grand scale. Jefferson had doubled the territory of his nation overnight, and guaranteed that it would have the space and resources to expand to great power status. But it came with several ironies.

First, the rule Jefferson imposed on the newly-incorporated territory was surprisingly despotic. He argued that this was a necessary step because the citizens were not ready for self-government, but critics then and later saw no justification behind this claim beyond Jefferson's own convenience. Dissatisfaction in these territories at this arrangement may be part of what later led Burr to believe he could form them into a new nation of his own.

Second, the sudden doubling of the United States meant that the horrific process of what would later be called Indian Removal could now begin in earnest. Before, the US had had no surplus territory on which to dispose of its unwanted peoples. Now the "Civilized Tribes" and "uncivilized" indigenous peoples alike would find themselves relentlessly marched west, often at gunpoint, away from their ancestral lands. Without the Louisiana Purchase, there could have been no Trail of Tears. Jefferson himself helped put these policies of Indian Removal in place. Though he believed that indigenous peoples could be assimilated with whites, assuming that they would abandon all vestiges of their own cultures, he also warned that, "if we are constrained to lift the hatchet against any tribe, we will never lay it down until that tribe is exterminated or driven beyond the Mississippi."

Lastly, the Purchase guaranteed the expansion of slavery into further territories. Until this point, the US had predominantly expanded into the northwest, where the Jefferson Proviso mandated that the new states ban slavery. Now the South would have room to expand as well, and would insist on remaining a voting bloc on par with the North, leaving the two on a collision course that could only be settled by war. Congress rejected an amendment similar to the Jefferson Proviso for the Louisiana Purchase, and this time Jefferson was silent on the issue. He was no longer trying to hold the line against slavery's expansion, and the cancer in the republic now grew unchecked.

## Lewis and Clark

Another positive outcome of the Louisiana Purchase was the famous Lewis and Clark expedition. Meriwether Lewis had long been a secretary of Jefferson's, and in 1803, Jefferson appointed him to head a Corps of Discovery to explore the newly acquired western territories and seek a route to the Pacific Ocean. Lewis' co-leader would be his good friend William Clark, an army lieutenant and experienced explorer.

In dispatching them, Jefferson had a range of motives. He wanted practical information on the strength of Spanish and Indian threats that lay within or beyond the new US borders. He sought scientific information about the species of the remote wilderness, and asked them to keep an eye out for mammoths—then a scientific mystery of which only a few bones existed. (Lewis and Clark found no mammoths, but they did have memorable encounters with such new species as prairie dogs and grizzly bears.) He wanted maps to help guide US expansion and commerce into the new region. And he wanted to establish an early US claim along the Pacific coast, already believed to be a site of potential confrontation with Britain.

Lewis and Clark's expedition was one of the great adventures of US history. They traveled 8,000 miles, from St. Louis to the Pacific Ocean and back, and published volume after volume of scientific and geographic observations. Clark's maps were the best of the region until the 1840s. Sadly, as with almost any white explorers of the nineteenth century, their legacy was tarnished by what followed in their wake. Lewis and Clark were generally respectful of indigenous cultures, and one of their guides, the Shoshone woman Sacajawea, would later become an American icon, even featured on US coinage. But they came as agents of a president and nation who believed in cultural, and sometimes physical, genocide for indigenous peoples. Within a century, every indigenous nation that Lewis and Clark visited would be stripped of its sovereignty and have its population devastated by disease, warfare, and starvation. For these peoples, the Corps of Discovery was only a foretaste of doom.

# Chapter 5: Burr, Embargo, and Disaster

# The Election of 1804

In 1804, the Federalist Party was in even greater disarray than in 1800. Like the Reconstruction Era Democrats in the South, the Federalists were now a mere regional party, with little strength outside of New England, watching the more populous party rule. The Democratic-Republicans would in fact hold office for twenty-four straight years—two terms for Jefferson, two for Madison, two for Monroe—until the 1824 election of John Adams' son, John Quincy. Federalists were hobbled by their aristocratic leanings and the rapidly expanding franchise; less and less property was required to vote in most states, and these voters understandably preferred the party that had enfranchised them in the first place, the Democratic-Republicans. The US population also continued to swell through immigration, and these voters, too, tended to prefer the more egalitarian party of the South.

Lastly, the "Virginian Dynasty" of presidents was greatly aided by a quirk of constitutional law, the "Three-Fifths Compromise." Southern delegates to the Constitutional Conventional had cheekily insisted that enslaved persons also be counted in a state's population, even though they would never be allowed to vote. The North balked, but finally agreed to count each slave as three-fifths of a person for purposes of assigning Congressional representation and Electoral College delegates. The slave population of the South continued to swell—in some states, enslaved blacks even outnumbered free whites—causing the South to take a disproportionate role in national affairs. Indeed, population estimates suggest that without the slave "vote" swelling Jefferson's support, Adams would have defeated him in 1800 and remained president.

After long deliberation, the Federalists nominated Charles C. Pinckney, a governor of South Carolina, in hopes of expanding outside of their regional appeal. On the Democratic-Republican side, Jefferson selected a new running mate, New York governor George Clinton—Edmond-Charles Genêt's father-in-law and another nemesis of Alexander Hamilton. But Burr was being replaced on the ticket for the very reason that Hamilton no longer existed, fatally shot through the side by Burr in a famous duel in New Jersey. Burr's disloyalty in 1800 might have caused him to be removed from the ticket in any case, but the murder of a fellow Founding Father—even if no legal action could be taken—sealed his fate. Burr headed west, but would soon be heard from again.

Meanwhile, Jefferson trounced Pinckney in the electoral contest. Buoyed by a booming economy and the triumphs of the Barbary War and Louisiana Purchase, the Democratic-Republican Party seemed unstoppable. Pinckney not only failed to win Southern support to the Federalist cause, he could not even hold New England, winning only Connecticut and Delaware, and 27% of the national popular vote.

It is a truism of American politics that a landslide re-election often precedes presidential hubris. Such was the case for Franklin D. Roosevelt, who followed his 1936 triumph over Alf Landon with his disastrous plan to "pack" the Supreme Court with friendly justices. Such was the case for Lyndon B. Johnson, who won a record landslide over Barry Goldwater in 1964 only to plunge the nation deeper and deeper into Vietnam. Such was the case for Ronald Reagan, who followed his decisive 1984 victory over Walter Mondale by attempting to circumvent Congress in the Iran-Contra Affair.

Such would be the case for Thomas Jefferson as well.

# Aaron Burr

Aaron Burr is one of the most fascinating Founding Fathers for the very reason that he is so much unlike the others. Hamilton, Jefferson, Madison, Adams, and the others were all deeply versed in constitutional history and law, and left extensive correspondence about their thinking on government. Jefferson and Madison's surviving letters alone require a three-volume collection totaling more than 2000 pages. Burr left no such theoretical musings, and appears to have had no real opinions beyond a raw desire for power.

Burr had made a name for himself during the disastrous invasion of Canada in the Revolutionary War (as with so many future American conflicts, the army was reassured by politicians that they would be greeted by Canadians as liberators), and then built a major power base as a lawyer and politician in New York, recognizing the Democratic-Republicans early on as the wave of the future. He personally created the Tammany Hall political machine that would become internationally notorious under Boss Tweed as well as a political enemy of both President Roosevelts early in their careers. Democratic-Republicans had added him to the ticket to deliver New York in 1796 and 1800—he failed the first time, succeeded the second—but by 1804, the Hamilton affair had finished him.

Whether Hamilton fired at Burr in the duel was disputed in every account then and since—one witness said yes, the other no—but what is certain is that Burr fired back, ending both his and Hamilton's political lives with a single bullet.

Ever restless, ever ambitious, however, Burr was not prepared to settle back into respectable legal practice. Instead, he began to reach out to a number of Jefferson's enemies with an audacious plan, the full extent of which historians are still struggling to uncover.

## Treason

The Louisiana Territory was the Wild West of its day, attracting adventurers, foreigners, wanderers, and general malcontents. The federal government had only a token presence in most parts of the region, and under

Jefferson's increasingly austere budgets, the US military was weaker than it had ever been before or would ever be again. Burr smelled opportunity.

He began recruitment for a large-scale military expedition—a "filibuster," in the parlance of the day. His partner was General James Wilkinson, the military governor for the Louisiana Territory. Wilkinson and Burr were old friends from the time of their Revolutionary Army service, and impressively, Wilkinson was the shadier of the two, simultaneously serving as a spy for the British, French, and Spanish in addition to his military duties and his plotting with Burr.

Where Burr and Wilkinson intended to take this force has never been conclusively resolved, and likely never will be. Burr hinted at many different plans to many different listeners and correspondents, though whether this was dishonesty or indecision remains unclear. At a minimum, he reached out to several foreign ministers for support in his armed venture, including Anthony Merry, the humorless, dour British minister who had nearly broken off diplomatic relations with the United States after Jefferson had intentionally snubbed his wife at a dinner party. (Merry was inclined to support Burr, but was recalled by a change of government in Britain before he could act.)

Some claimed that Burr planned not an attack on US territory, but to venture into Texas or another Spanish territory, seize control, and establish himself as a military dictator. Other historians believe, and this seems the most likely, that Burr would attempt to take control of part of the newly bought, sparsely settled Louisiana Territory. With the US Army presence loyal to him through Wilkinson, the two could establish their own empire on the United States' western border. It's also possible that Burr intended to do both of these things, or even take his army and march on Washington to seize control of the nation. On hearing the first reports of Burr's treachery, Jefferson feared the latter.

# The Trial of the Century

Jefferson ordered Burr's arrest on November 26, 1806. It was Wilkinson who ultimately betrayed Burr and would be the chief witness against him. As with all the actions of this quintuple-agent, his motives for doing so remain uncertain. Most likely, he recognized Burr's diminishing probability of success and hoped that by revealing the plot to Jefferson, he could forestall his own arrest for treason.

Burr was arrested in January 1807, released by a grand jury in the Louisiana Territory, but re-arrested in February while attempting to flee. Jefferson then made the first great blunder of his second term, issuing a statement to Congress that Burr's "guilt is placed beyond question." It was an unwise statement in so murky a situation, and placed Jefferson in the unfortunate position of having a measure of his prestige staked on the trial's outcome. He began to oversee the prosecution's case against Burr personally and wrote reams of letters to persuade others of Burr's guilt. Even before it began, the case became a national sensation—one needs only picture Dick Cheney or Joe Biden on trial for conspiracy and attempted rebellion to imagine the national uproar.

Unfortunately for Jefferson, the case was tried in federal court, and Supreme Court Chief Justice John Marshall, his long-time foe, would be presiding. Marshall dismissed the treason charge as having insufficient evidence, establishing an important precedent that guaranteed treason charges would be rare in American political life. Jefferson and his party were enraged, though historians have since seen Marshall as doing the country a valuable service in forestalling the abuse of such charges. Indeed, in the centuries since, only a handful of individuals have ever been convicted on federal treason charges: the abolitionist raider John Brown, the World War II broadcaster "Tokyo Rose," the conspirators in the Lincoln assassination, Julius and Ethel Rosenberg, and less than a dozen others.

Another important precedent was set when Burr boldly subpoenaed Jefferson himself. Jefferson's papers held nothing to exonerate Burr, but Burr apparently hoped to discover damaging or embarrassing information that would help him in the court of public opinion. Jefferson compromised by allowing court officials to see relevant documents, but cited "executive privilege" to prevent their public release. This sensible doctrine held that presidents could not fulfill their duties, particularly diplomacy, without a modicum of secrecy; it would be both used and abused by many future presidents, most notably in Richard Nixon's final attempt to prevent release of his Oval Office recordings.

Ultimately, the jury found Burr not guilty on all charges. Wilkinson, on whom so much of the government's case depended, had fallen apart under cross-examination and shown himself to be the utterly unreliable witness that he was. Though Burr had clearly been up to something and probably deserved jail or even hanging, the evidence was still too hazy to convict him of any individual charge.

Jefferson denounced the verdict, and Marshall joined the long list of Federalist figures burned in effigy by Democratic-Republican mobs. But Jefferson had no real cards left to play, and in any case, he now needed every ounce of his remaining political capital to deal with the worsening international situation.

Burr returned to New York to practice law, outliving Jefferson by a decade. Even at the end of his life, he remained a prominent and controversial figure; in 1836, the year of his death, a widely circulated rumor held him to be the biological father of presidential candidate Martin Van Buren.

## Impressment and Trade

The Napoleonic Wars continued to roil the oceans throughout Jefferson's second term. One growing problem was the issue of "impressment," the British euphemism for the kidnapping of sailors to be forced to serve in their navy. It's a great historical irony that while the abolitionist movement seeking to end chattel slavery was reaching its height in Britain, so too was the practice of kidnapping white men for forced labor on British warships.

Many of the men thus seized later sought to escape their "service" and found refuge in the American merchant marine; Jefferson's Treasury Secretary Albert Gallatin himself estimated that as many as one-third of American sailors were deserters from the British Navy. British captains began regularly stopping and searching American ships, and drafting anyone thought to be British back into their service as a presumed deserter. The United States and Britain had only been separate nations for a few decades now, and these distinctions were not easy to assess on sight. Many mistakes were made, and the anger of the American public grew.

But Britain was unwilling to compromise. Its fleet was the only thing stopping Napoleon from invading the British Isles, where British forces would be unlikely to win a land war against the brilliant general. Despite increasing diplomatic protests, the British searches of American ships continued.

These ships also searched American vessels for contraband, which in essence meant any goods being shipped to Napoleon-dominated Europe. Between 1805 and 1806, the cargoes of one out of every eight American merchant ships were being confiscated by the British. The French, too, sought to confiscate American shipments to Britain, but its fleet was largely confined to port after the decisive

British naval victory at Trafalgar in 1805. French seizures thus had much less impact on the popular consciousness. 1500 American ships were taken by the two powers between 1803 and 1812, with Britain claiming about two-thirds of that total.

Jefferson requested that some of the navy he had ordered dismantled now be reconstructed. Congressional Federalists, who feared any interruption of trade with Britain, and some Democratic-Republicans, many of whom were now far more radical than their president, refused. But Congress did agree to a "Non-Importation Act" as a punishment for Britain, a mild example of what we would today call "sanctions." The Non-Importation Act was not scheduled to begin immediately, but in nine months, in hopes that the British would respond favorably to the pressure and make the issue moot. This act abrogated Jay's

Treaty, which had guaranteed free commercial exchange between the two nations, but Jefferson had always despised this forced link with Britain and welcomed the chance to be rid of it.

He dispatched Monroe and William Pinkney to London to negotiate a new treaty, but neither side was willing to give ground. Britain proved unwilling to budge on the impressment issue, while Monroe and Pinkney had been instructed not to give up the United States' right to embargo British shipping. Monroe and Pinkney returned with a draft treaty that might have calmed relations, but did little to address the underlying issues. Jefferson declined to submit it to the Senate.

# The Chesapeake–Leopard Affair

On June 22, 1807, the USS Chesapeake was leaving the eponymous bay, destined for the Mediterranean and yet another round of combat against the Barbary States. But not far from shore, the British warship HMS Leopard intercepted the Chesapeake and demanded to board to search for deserters. The Chesapeake's captain, James Barron, refused. The Leopard opened fire with its complement of fifty guns, killing three American sailors and wounding many more; the unprepared Chesapeake only got off one shot in response. The Leopard boarded and took away four men as "deserters," three of whom proved to actually be Americans.

The public howled with outrage at the British arrogance and the Chesapeake's poor showing. Jefferson wrote that "Never since the Battle of Lexington have I seen this country in such a state of exasperation as at present, and even that did not produce such unanimity." Captain Barron was court-martialed and suspended from service for five years; he would later briefly re-enter history when he killed America's preeminent naval hero, Stephen Decatur, in a duel over Decatur's comments on his conduct.

# Embargo

Jefferson began to prepare for war. He laid plans to invade Canada (a pipe dream the United States would not abandon until 1812) and to fortify the nation's coast.

But Congress balked. Jefferson's Democratic-Republican ideology had taken root too well, even as Jefferson now drifted back toward the center. His requests for additional gunboats were refused even as the country demanded a substantial response to British aggression. For their part, the British were not eager for another front in the Napoleonic Wars, and offered both an apology and reparations, but still refused to abandon the policy of impressment.

Like many politicians to follow, Jefferson eventually crafted a compromise that combined the worst of all possible alternatives. He always had an inflated idea of America's global role, and this vision had led him to many of his finest moments in public life. But now it led to disaster.

Between them, Jefferson and Madison developed a plan to embargo all shipping between Europe and the United States, reasoning that this would cripple the economies of both Britain and France. Once both nations had felt the pinch, they would be forced to quickly settle their conflict; America would thus lead the way to a new era of global peace. Gallatin, always more practical on money matters, tried to persuade Jefferson to abandon the scheme as delusional or even declare war instead, but Jefferson saw an opportunity to put another of his cherished ideals into practice. He would not be moved.

On December 22, 1807, at Jefferson's request, Congress passed the Embargo Act with little debate. In the words of historian Gordon S. Wood, "perhaps never in history has a trading nation of America's size engaged in such an act of self-immolation with so little reward."

# Uprising

The embargo was ill-conceived from the start. France had no need of American trade, as it was growing wealthy from Napoleon's "Continental System," which forced conquered European nations to trade with France but banned them from trading with Britain. Britain's economy was far larger than that of the United States, and could survive far worse blows than the loss of one of its many trading partners. The Napoleonic Wars continued as if nothing had happened.

At home, however, the consequences were devastating. American trade dropped by as much as 75% overnight, demolishing whole sectors of the economy. Ships sat empty and unmoving in the harbors, and America's first attempts at a manufacturing sector now had nowhere to send their goods. New England, always far more commercial than the South, was particularly hard-hit, to the outrage of the Federalists. Hate mail and even death threats began to arrive for Jefferson from around the country.

Rather than admit his failure, Jefferson doubled down. Smuggling was rife on a scale that would not be seen again until Prohibition, and Jefferson asked Congress to authorize a large force to police American violations of the embargo, particularly in New England. The Canadian border was a particular source of trouble; Jefferson finally declared the region to be in open insurrection and dispatched the US Army to keep order.

Jefferson's about-face on so many issues astounded observers then and has continued to surprise historians ever since. Here was the architect of the "nullification" doctrine, asserting the right of the federal government to entirely halt a state's trade; here was the man who had been enraged to see even Shays's Rebellion put down, dispatching the army to pacify an entire region. As biographer R. B. Bernstein points out, Jefferson was now "pursuing policies resembling those he had cited in 1776 as grounds for independence and revolution." When he declared Massachusetts to be in "rebellion," however, Jefferson seemed oblivious to the irony that this was precisely the sort of rebellion he had supported throughout his life.

## The End of the Embargo

Federalists began to mount a more and more organized resistance to the embargo. States like Massachusetts and Connecticut began to espouse doctrines much like Jefferson's own nullification, and there was even talk by a few hot-headed legislators of breaking away from the Union. Democratic-Republicans held the line for a time, but the economic carnage wrought by the policy was increasingly obvious even to Jefferson's own supporters.

Jefferson held his ground to the end, believing his policy to be the world's best chance at a lasting peace. Even later in life, he would maintain that the embargo could have ended the war if only it been more strictly observed; unfortunately, it had been undermined by the usual cabal of moneyed interests and "monocrats."

Always unable to tolerate sustained conflict, Jefferson retreated from public life for most of the last year of his presidency, even as the Union threatened to tear itself apart. Madison and Gallatin were given charge of most affairs, while Jefferson took an extended vacation to

Monticello. Politicians of both parties muttered about the president washing his hands of the disaster like Pontius Pilate.

Despite the embargo disaster, the Federalists still proved unable to take states outside of New England, and in November 1808, James Madison was elected as Jefferson's successor. Jefferson had mentally departed the capital some months before, and his physical departure now was only a formality. He compared himself to "a prisoner, released from his chains."

The embargo was ended by Congress on Madison's first day in office.

# Chapter 6: Retirement and Legacy

# The War of 1812

The mischief of Jefferson's embargo act did not end with his presidency, however. Relations between the United States and Britain had deteriorated dramatically during the embargo, both because of continued impressment and confiscation, and because Republican authors and orators blamed Britain rather than Jefferson for the joblessness and poverty now afflicting so many Americans. Madison unwisely continued to press Jefferson's complaints, and declared war against the world's greatest naval power in 1812, just as Britain agreed to accede to American demands on impressment.

The nation was very lucky to escape undefeated and intact. The war was only a sideshow for Britain, a curious additional theater in the Napoleonic Wars. British forces nonetheless successfully raided Washington, D.C. and burned the White House; needless to say, Madison was not able to launch a similar assault on Buckingham Palace. British raiders struck all along the southern coast, burning plantations and fomenting small-scale slave rebellions. Early American naval victories were offset after Napoleon's first defeat, freeing up more of the superior British navy for duty in the Western Hemisphere. Neither Jefferson nor Madison had had the political will to force their Democratic-Republican allies to approve the needed levels of military strength, and the United States simply was not ready for the fight.

Meanwhile, New England had been brought into the war against its will and made no secret of the fact. The talk of secession begun by Jefferson's embargo rose to new heights, and in 1814, the Hartford Convention met in

Connecticut to discuss breaking away from the United States. Only the war's sudden end—and the pleasant surprise of a last-minute victory at New Orleans by General Andrew Jackson—stopped the situation from becoming a constitutional crisis.

These events occurred on Madison's watch, not Jefferson's, and he deserves the lion's share of the blame. But the seeds of the disaster—the lack of preparedness, the escalation of international tensions, the exacerbation of regional hostilities, and the evisceration of the American economy—were all planted by Jefferson in his final term. Madison only continued to water them.

## Jefferson in Retirement

Jefferson was now retired, and would never return to public life in a significant way. Being

Jefferson, of course, his final two decades were devoted not to leisure, but to the sort of pursuits he could not find time for as president. He spent hours every day at his desk composing letters; in terms of sheer written output, it is unlikely that any American leader could ever compete with him. He refocused his attention on attempts to reorganize Monticello and get the estate out of debt, though with characteristic avoidance of unpleasant topics, he spent less and less time around his slaves, preferring to deal with them through intermediaries.

Jefferson was kind to his enslaved workers by the standards of his day. They were rarely beaten, and he avoided breaking up families wherever possible. When he did sell slaves, it was often at their request to reunite them with family members. But they were enslaved nonetheless, and their own feelings about their captivity can be surmised by the repeated advertisements that Jefferson placed seeking the recapture of runaways.

It's unclear whether Jefferson seriously considered freeing his slaves at his death. He surely knew how harshly history would judge him for owning slaves, and George Washington had already set an example by freeing his own slaves in his will. But thanks to Jefferson's hopeless indebtedness, his property was no longer his to dispose of as he pleased. Even now, with the red growing in his ledger and the final disposal of his property soon to be a reality, Jefferson was unable to refrain from spending lavishly on food, foreign wine, and new books. To settle one set of outstanding debts, he persuaded Congress to buy his entire collection of books, which formed the nucleus of the future Library of Congress. Yet Jefferson simply used the money to begin purchasing a new library for his home, and new construction on Monticello continued all the while.

In the end, Jefferson would be able to free only Sally Hemings' siblings and children. Hemings herself was not freed in Jefferson's will, but as Annette Gordon-Reed points out, this is likely due to her age; the Virginia legislature prevented older slaves being freed without special dispensation to prevent owners from simply turning out their disabled or elderly workers. Instead, Hemings was "given her time," meaning that she was exempted from work and could travel freely, or at least as freely as any African American could under Virginia's strict codes. She settled in Charlottesville with two of her and Thomas' sons.

# The University of Virginia

One long-standing dream of Jefferson's was a public, secular university founded on Enlightenment ideals. Almost all the universities of his day were religious institutions, often dedicated primarily to training clergy, associated with particular sects or creeds. He had first written of the dream to fellow philosophe Joseph Priestley in 1800, but it was not until 1819, when Jefferson was 76, that the University was finally established by the Virginia legislature.

Jefferson was active in every aspect of the university's development. He secured the necessary state and private funds—for obvious reasons, Jefferson could make little contribution himself—and guaranteed that its charter would be secular. He designed the grounds, the buildings, and the rotunda of its library. He served as its first rector in 1825, though at this point Jefferson was only a year away from death and his duties were mostly ceremonial. (As in so many other things, he would be succeeded in the post by his lifelong partner, James Madison.)

## Final Years

Beyond his work with the university, Jefferson spent much of his last decades trying to secure his place in history. As one of the last major revolutionary figures to die, he had ample opportunity to do so. He reviewed and revised some of his correspondence, particularly some of his more exuberant paeans to the French Revolution and some of his more duplicitous letters to Federalists or Burr. He wrote most of an autobiography, though he did not live to complete it. (Frustratingly for future generations of scholars, he made no attempts to fill in the lacunae of his childhood left by the Shadwell fire, focusing only on his adult life.) He made an appearance with the Marquis de Lafayette when that noble triumphantly toured America in 1825, massive crowds greeting him at every stop. He even renewed his friendship with John and Abigail Adams, and though the two former presidents never saw one another again, they exchanged hundreds of letters in which they reflected on the history and philosophies of the American Revolution. This extraordinary exchange between former political rivals has no equal in American history, and Joseph J. Ellis has called it "the intellectual capstone to the achievements of the revolutionary generation."

Extraordinarily, Adams and Jefferson managed to die on the same day, July 4, 18266, the fiftieth anniversary of the signing of the

Declaration of Independence to the very day. (Both men, it must be said, were clearly aiming for it—the dying Jefferson repeatedly asked the family at his bedside if it was yet the fourth. "Is it the Fourth?" would prove to be the last sentence he ever uttered.) In Massachusetts, Adams gasped out among his dying words, "Thomas Jefferson survives," but Jefferson had in fact preceded him into death by several hours. Adams' son John Quincy was then the sitting president, and proclaimed that the extraordinary coincidence showed the hand of God in the nation's affairs.

Thomas Jefferson left a fair amount of debt to his inheritors, and the following years would see a great sell-off of Monticello's lands and slaves, save for the Hemings family. He also left precise instructions for the marker he wanted over his grave at Monticello. It was to be a tall obelisk, and made of granite, not marble, to deter theft. Even this measure proved hopeless; so many tourists chiseled off a piece as a souvenir that Congress had to order a new one constructed sixty years later. The original now stands at the University of Missouri–Columbia.

The instructions also included the epitaph, in which Jefferson listed the three achievements by which he wished history to remember him:

> *Here was buried*
> *Thomas Jefferson*
> *Author of the Declaration of American*
> *Independence*
> *of the Statute of Virginia for religious freedom*
> *& Father of the University of Virginia*

His two terms as president—which had so divided and, in the end, damaged the nation—were not mentioned at all.

# Sources

Bernstein, R. B. Thomas Jefferson. Oxford: Oxford University Press, 2003.

Borneman, Walter R. 1812: The War that Forged a Nation. New York: Harper Collins, 2004.

Cerami, Charles A. Jefferson's Great Gamble: The Remarkable Story of Jefferson, Napoleon and the Men Behind the Louisiana Purchase. Napierville: Sourcebooks, Inc., 2003.

Chernow, Ron. Alexander Hamilton. New York: Penguin, 2005.

Crawford, Alan Pell. Twilight at Monticello: The Final Years of Thomas Jefferson. New York: Random House, 2008.

Cunningham, Noble E. In Pursuit of Reason: The Life of Thomas Jefferson. Baton Rouge: Louisiana State University Press, 1987.

Ellis, Joseph J. American Creation: Triumphs and Tragedies at the Founding of the Republic. New York: 2007.

----. American Sphinx: The Character of Thomas Jefferson. New York: Knopf, 1998.

----. Founding Brothers: The Revolutionary Generation. New York: Vintage, 2000.

Ferling, John. Jefferson and Hamilton: The Rivalry that Forged a Nation. New York: Bloomsbury Press, 2013.

Gordon-Reed, Annette. The Hemingses of Monticello: An American Family. New York: W.W. Norton, 2008.

Herring, George C. From Colony to Superpower: U.S. Foreign Relations Since 1776. Oxford: Oxford University Press, 2008.

Hyland, Jr., William G. Martha Jefferson: An Intimate Life with Thomas Jefferson. Lanham: Rowman & Littlefield, 2015.

Jefferson, Thomas. Notes on the State of Virginia. New York: Penguin, 1998.

Jefferson, Thomas and Madison, James. The Republic of Letters: The Collected Correspondence Between Thomas Jefferson and James Madison. Ed. James Morton Smith. New York: W. W. Norton & Co., 1995.

Kennedy, Roger G. Mr. Jefferson's Lost Cause: Land, Farmers, Slavery, and the Louisiana Purchase. Oxford: Oxford University Press, 2003.

Kilmeade, Brian and Don Yaeger. Thomas Jefferson and the Tripoli Pirates: The Forgotten War that Changed American History. New York: Penguin, 2015.

McCullough, David. John Adams. New York: Simon & Schuster, 2001.

Middlekauff, Robert. The Glorious Cause: The American Revolution, 1763-1789. Oxford: Oxford University Press, 2005.

Slack, Charles. Liberty's First Crisis: Adams, Jefferson, and the Misfits Who Saved Free Speech. New York: Atlantic Monthly Press, 2015.

Staloff, Darren. Hamilton, Adams, Jefferson: The Politics of Enlightenment and the American Founding. New York: Farrar, Strauss, and Giroux, 2005.

Vidal, Gore. Inventing a Nation: Washington, Adams, Jefferson. New Haven: Yale University Press, 2005.

Wood, Gordon S. Empire of Liberty: A History of the Early Republic, 1789-1815. Oxford: Oxford University Press, 2009

Made in the USA
Middletown, DE
13 July 2018